3 0250 01064 1780
D0767828

MERI REPORT KUWAIT

MERI REPORT

KUWAIT

Middle East Research Institute
University of Pennsylvania

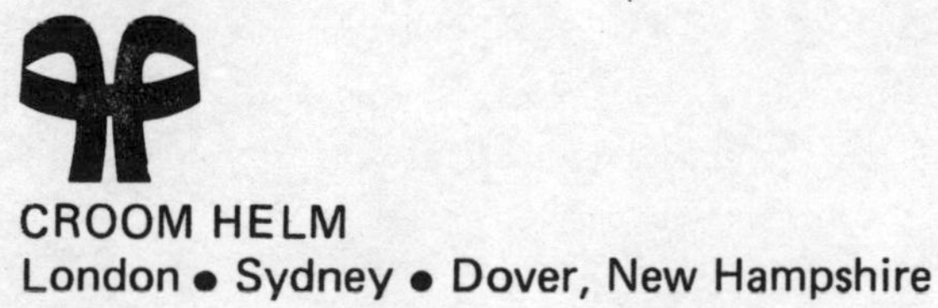

CROOM HELM
London • Sydney • Dover, New Hampshire

Croom Helm Ltd, Provident House , Burrell Row,
Beckenham, Kent BR3 1AT

Croom Helm Australia Pty Ltd, First Floor,
139 King Street, Sydney, NSW 2001, Australia

British Library Cataloguing in Publication Data

Kuwait. – (Meri report)
1. Kuwait – Social conditions
I. University of Pennsylvania. *Middle East Research Institute* II. Series
953'.67053 HN669.A8

ISBN 0-7099-3546-3

Croom Helm, 51 Washington Street, Dover,
New Hampshire 03820, USA

Library of Congress Cataloging in Publication Data

University of Pennsylvania. Middle East Research
Institute.
MERI report, Kuwait.

1. Kuwait. 2. Kuwait – Economic conditions. I. Title.
II. Title: M.E.R.I. report, Kuwait.
DS247.K8U65 1985 330.953'67053 84-28552
ISBN 0-7099-3546-3 (pbk.)

Printed and bound in Great Britain by
Antony Rowe Ltd., Chippenham

TABLE OF CONTENTS

Transportation & Communications

Health, Education and Welfare

I. BACKGROUND

1. GEOGRAPHY. The State of Kuwait, an area of about 17,818 sq km (1 sq km = 0.386 sq mi) of mostly flat desert, is in the northwestern corner of the Persian Gulf and has one of the few natural harbors (Kuwait Bay) in the northern portion of the Gulf. There are 499 km of coastline. Iraq lies to the north and northwest, Saudi Arabia to the south and southwest, and the Gulf directly to the east. Very little vegetation grows outside the populated areas. Scrub brush is found along the salt flats near the shore, and small thorn bushes are scattered throughout the interior and in the few wadis. There is a small oasis, al-Jahrah, located 96 km west of Kuwait City.

The Neutral Zone, (5,700 sq km) was partitioned between Kuwait and Saudi Arabia in 1966; revenue from oil production in the zone is shared between both countries.

2. CLIMATE. The temperature is very hot in the summer, ranging from 29.7° to 45.1° C (85° to 113° F). In the winter, this ranges from 8.4° to 18.4° C (46° to 66° F), with occasional drops below freezing at night but warming up in the daytime.

Although Kuwait has an overall desert climate, there are occasional winter rains, bringing grass and small purple flowers to the desert in early spring. Annual rainfall varies between 10 and 350 mm, most of which falls within the winter months of November-March (1 mm = 0.039 inch). Sandstorms are frequent in the summer. Humidity, although somewhat lower than in neighboring Bahrain, aggravates the severe summer heat, making air conditioning a necessity.

3. POPULATION. The estimated population of Kuwait, according to the 1980 census, was 1.36 million. Of this number, approximately 41.5 percent are Kuwaiticitizens (officially defined as those present in Kuwait prior to 1920, their descendants, and a relatively small number of persons given Kuwaiti citizenship).

Both the Kuwaiti and non-Kuwaiti populations have grown rapidly; the Kuwaiti population has one of the highest growth rates in the world (about 4.5 percent from 1975 to 1980). The non-Kuwaiti population has an unusually high proportion of young and middle-aged adult males, many in construction and service jobs. The foreign population consists primarily of workers (sometimes accompanied by their families) who are in Kuwait to take advantage of the relatively high wages and the shortage of labor in all areas of employment. Jobs held by immigrants range from manual labor to important government and managerial positions. Palestinians and Jordanians make up about 22 percent of the total population; Egyptians, 4 percent; other Arabs, about 15 percent; Iranians, Pakistanis, and Indians, about ten percent; and the remaining two percent come from Eastern and Western Europe, the Americas, and the Far East.

The population is relatively young; 58.3 percent are less than 25 years old. The population density is 80.2 per sq km.

4. RESOURCES. Except for the natural source of drinking water at Raudhatain, 96 km north of the capital, Kuwait has virtually no water resources. It depends upon desalination techniques to provide drinking water and water for industry. Some groundwater reservoirs have been found but most of these are brackish.

Arable land is scarce, representing only about one percent of the total area. The lack of water, combined with the poor quality of the soil, makes agriculture almost impossible, except for small plots.

Before the discovery of oil, Kuwaitis looked to the sea for fishing, pearling and maritime trading for their livelihood. In the past, fresh water was obtained from springs under the sea by divers who would trap it in jugs and bring it to the surface. The sea is an important source for Kuwait of shrimp and fish, which are sold for local consumption and export. In the late 1970s Kuwaiti officials became concerned about industrial pollution in the Gulf and permanent damage to the shrimp and fish habitats. Kuwait has pressed for agreement on action among the Gulf states, although no such agreement has yet been reached. The government has for several years funded research and experimentation in commercial shrimp farming. Kuwait has also experimented for some time with hydroponics and animal husbandry in order to reduce dependence on imported foodstuffs. Fishing and agriculture in Kuwait require government support to survive; neither industry has been able to attract many Kuwaitis due to the more lucrative opportunities in the petroleum and commercial sectors.

Kuwait's hydrocarbon resources (controlled by three government companies) make discussion of other natural resources almost a footnote. At the present production level of one mbd, Kuwait's oil reserves (approximately 68.53 billion barrels) are estimated to last for another 188 years. Moreover, production costs are low because the oil lies fairly close to the surface; an optimum geological formation results in a natural gravity flow which all but runs the oil directly into the tankers. While a barrel of Kuwaiti oil sells for $29, a U.S. Department of Energy official has estimated its cost of production to be about 25 cents. Crude oil reserves, the efficient use of associated gas, the potential for development and export of unassociated gas, and the manufacture and export of petrochemicals from crude oil insure Kuwait's financial well-being far into the future.

The Kuwaiti leadership has always faced the political and economic problem of how much crude oil to produce. Over the past three years, the production level has been reduced from two mbd in 1979 to just under one mbd in 1983. This decision reflects the current oil glut, as well as a response to nationalist-minded Arabs, both in and out of Kuwait, to conserve their natural resources. Kuwait, with its small population and relatively small development needs, has an income more than sufficient for domestic spending, for maintenance of a large investment program, and for a generous foreign aid plan. One constraint on too severe a cut in production, whether desired or forced by events such as the oil glut, is the Kuwaiti policy of using associated gas to fire domestic industry. Since associated gas is related to oil production, there is a minimum oil production required in order to maintain sufficient gas supplies.

5. SOCIAL STRUCTURE. The nomadic way of life is dying out in Kuwait, as it is elsewhere. Bedouin are joining the mainstream of Kuwaiti society in large numbers but are still not full participants in business, political, and social life. For those Bedouin who formerly migrated back and forth between the Fertile Crescent and the Arabian Peninsula, military service is a way of assuming both Kuwaiti citizenship and full participation in Kuwaiti social programs.

Although pastoralism is diminishing in Kuwait, tribal and extended family loyalties are the basic building blocks of Kuwaiti society. The self-identity of most native Kuwaitis is based on the extended family and larger kinship groups. These loyalities are important not only in a social sense but also in a political sense in that blood ties are the predominant determinant of Kuwaiti citizenship and membership in the political elite.

The most prominent Kuwaitis are descendents of the Bani Utub (People who Wandered), who migrated to Kuwait early in the 17th century from central Arabia. The Bani Utub took advantage of tribal warfare in northeast Arabia to assert their independence in the 1750s, with a member of the Al Sabah family being chosen as shaikh. The political leadership of Kuwait has rested with the Al Sabah ever since. Although of nomadic origin, the Bani Utub quickly took to such occupations as pearling, fishing, and maritime commerce. Eventually, power in Kuwait came to be held by a merchant aristocracy, with the most prominent families being the Al Sabah, al-Ghani, al-Janat, al-Saqr, and al-Salih. As traditional Kuwait prospered as a regional entrepot, other Arab and non-Arab groups settled in the emirate. There is a sizeable Shiite community in Kuwait, estimated at approximately 15-20 percent of the total population and including both Arab and Persian elements with relatives in Iraq, Saudi Arabia, and Bahrain.

Although the merchant families that dominated the economy before the discovery of petroleum have benefited from the new oil wealth, they have lost considerable influence to the ruling family, whose power has grown tremendously because it controls the oil wealth, and therefore the economy. The educational system has removed the social barriers to white collar occupations, and native-born laborers, as a class, are being replaced by foreigners.

Women enjoy considerable freedom in Kuwait. Kuwaiti women travel widely, study overseas, and participate in commercial and financial life. Although there are no Kuwaiti women in the highest ranking government positions, a number of important mid-level jobs are held by women and Kuwaiti women often represent their government at international conferences.

6. RELIGION. The majority of Kuwait's population is Sunni Muslim. There is a fairly large Shiite Muslim population and Kuwait has been tolerant of other religious minorities within its borders, Christians and Hindus among others. The Iranian revolution, which has struck a responsive chord among Shiites and Sunnis, continues to be a source of concern to the authorities. Islamic resurgence has made itself felt in more devout religious observance, as well as in expressions of political viewpoints and a desire to reinstate traditional Islamic values which have been undermined by commercialism and Westernization.

7. POLITICAL STRUCTURE AND LEADERSHIP. Kuwait is a constitutional monarchy, the rulers of which have been traditionally chosen from the Al Sabah family. The Constitution provides for a tripartite governmental structure. The Emir is head of state and is assisted by an 18-member cabinet which he appoints. A 50-member National Assembly, elected to a four-year term, has legislative functions. An independent judiciary constitutes the third branch of government. Candidates for the National Assembly are elected by a very narrow electoral base. Suffrage is restricted to literate male adults who are able to prove that their families were resident in Kuwait in 1920.

Despite these restrictions on eligibility, the National Assembly has always been a vocal forum for criticism of the government on domestic, regional and international issues. It was influenced by Nasser's principles of Arab nationalism, often in direct opposition to official Kuwaiti policies which favored appeasing Iraq in its conflict with Egypt. By 1976, overt criticism of neighboring countries caused the Emir to view the Assembly as a disruptive influence, and on August 29, 1976, he dissolved it. In February 1980 the government appointed a committee to review the Constitution and report in six months. Elections for the National Assembly were held in February, 1981. Victory went to the right, with the leftist Arab Nationalist Movement totally defeated. A small group of Sunni Muslim fundamentalists won four seats and are viewed as the only opposition group.

The monarchy in Kuwait is a traditional hereditary rulership. Succession as Emir is restricted to the heirs of Mubarak Al Sabah. Leadership alternates between two branches of the family, the Al Salim and the Al Jabir, named for the two sons of Mubarak Al Sabah, although this pattern was broken in 1966, when a Salim succeeded another Salim. Although politics in Kuwait revolve around the activities of the royal family, real power is shared with prominent groups in society such as the merchants, principal tribal groups, intelligentsia, technocrats and the ulema (religious leaders).

Political parties are forbidden in Kuwait; however, several groups – the Arab Nationalist Movement, the Baath, and various Palestinian groups – operate clandestinely.

In the past, the Arab Nationalist Movement has managed to gain seats in the National Assembly. The political groups or societies have access to the press as a forum for their ideas through members who are on the staffs of Kuwait's papers.

8. MILITARY STRUCTURE. Kuwait's military has two functions: to insure internal security and to slow down an aggressor long enough for diplomacy or allies to come to the country's aid. The Emir heads the nation's military structure. The Minister of Defense directs the army, the air force and the national guard through the army chief of staff. The minister of Interior directs the public security forces, the police and the coast guard. The top military posts are held by members of the Al Sabah family. Kuwait now has a small army of three brigades, with 10,000 troops. The air force has undergone rapid growth, acquiring sophisticated high-technology equipment such as Mirage and Skyhawk aircraft and Hawk surface-to-air missiles. There are 1,900 men in the air force. In proportion to total government expenditure, Kuwait spent 7.8 percent on defense in 1983. Most of the weapons and technical expertise are French, British or U.S. in origin, although in recent years the regime has turned to the USSR for supplies. In July 1984, an agreement was signed with the Soviet Union to provide both arms and military training.

9. FOREIGN RELATIONS. The foreign policy ofKuwait has been shaped by a number of factors, including Kuwait's geographical position at the head of the Gulf, regional politics, and its oil resources used as a tool of foreign aid.

Geography. Kuwait became independent of Britain in 1961, and was threatened almost immediately by Iraqi claims to sovereignty. First British, then Arab League forces were sent to maintain Kuwaiti independence. Iraq dropped its claims in 1963 after the fall of the Qassim regime and the payment of a substantial grant. Border problems which flared in 1973 provided the impetus for major expansion of the Kuwaiti armed forces. Geographical considerations and a fear of Iranian appeals to Shiite minorities influenced Kuwait's decision in 1980 to back Iraq in the Gulf War. The war was a key factor in the establishment in 1981 of the Gulf Cooperation Council to foster military, economic and cultural cooperation among the Gulf states.

Regional Politics. Kuwait's regional influence has grown significantly since it began to use its revenues for Arab, particularly Palestinian, causes. At the same time, it no longer supports either Syria or the radical factions of the PLO. It contributed heavily to the reconstruction effort in Jordan and Egypt following the 1967 war. In 1973, Kuwait called the OAPEC meeting which led to the oil boycott, and was among the first states to raise prices unilaterally. Since then, it has been among the more hawkish oil producers regarding oil prices, although it has generally abided by its OPEC quotas.

Throughout the 1970s, Kuwait has maintained a consistent verbal commitment to Arab nationalism and Palestinian statehood. This stance is enforced not only by deference to more militant neighbors, but also by the presence in Kuwait of a large community of Palestinians who, although economically secure, do not hold Kuwaiti citizenship and hence are a source of domestic discontent.

Superpower Relations. Kuwait has sought to maintain a non-aligned position between the superpowers, and is the only GCC country to have diplomatic ties, and now military purchase agreements, with both the USA and the Soviet Union. Kuwait disapproves of the overtly pro-American policy of states such as Oman, and has lobbied other GCC countries to establish diplomatic ties with the eastern bloc. Kuwait's position as a major oil producer within OPEC has given it a certain degree of clout vis-a-vis western countries, and it has diversified its source of arms and contractors to reduce dependence on any one supplier.

Foreign Aid and the Third World. The Kuwaiti Fund for Arab Economic Development (KFAED) was formed in 1961, and since then has provided considerable development assistance to Jordan, Egypt, Syria, and other Arab, Muslim, and Third World countries. From 1975 through 1980, Kuwait gave $1.188 billion in development grants and loans, or 3.88 percent of its GNP. Preference for Kuwaiti aid appears to go to countries that share Kuwait's opposition to Israel.

10. ECONOMIC STRUCTURE. Hydrocarbons, particularly oil, dominate Kuwait's industry, contributing 49 percent of the GDP in 1982. Kuwait's oil revenues in 1980 were more than $18 billion. Of total exports, 90 percent were oil, refined petroleum products, and gas in 1980. The absence of raw materials other than hydrocarbons and a lack of skilled labor limits Kuwait's industrial development to oil-related industries (gas liquefication, petrochemicals, and refining). Although Kuwait cut oil production considerably in 1981, further cuts are unlikely since associated natural gas is the energy basis of most of the country's domestic development. The government controls hydrocarbon interests through three state-owned companies, one responsible for oil and gas production, one for internal distribution and international marketing, and one for petroleum-related products, particularly fertilizer. The main industrial centers are at Mina al-Abdullah and Shuaiba.

Due to oil price increases, the Kuwait government has amassed huge surpluses of foreign reserves. Most of these funds are invested abroad. Kuwait's reserve funds totaled $72 billion in 1983.

Agricultural development is severely limited due to the scarcity of water, high summer temperatures, and an infertile soil base. At present it accounts for less than 0.2 percent of the GNP. The government is making efforts to encourage vegetable and poultry farming in order to reduce its dependence on imported foodstuffs.

The non-oil industrial sector is still of limited importance. Boat building and construction are the most important industries within that sector. Domestic trade contributes nine percent of the GDP, manufacturing seven percent, and financial institutions five percent. Entrepot trade and pearl fishing have declined in importance with the development of the oil industry.

11. INFRASTRUCTURE. The building of infrastructure has been a major priority for Kuwait since the early days of independence, with the result that most infrastructure development is now complete.

Transportation. Transportation in Kuwait is generally good, with roads connecting most population and industrial centers. In 1980, there were 2,545 km of roads. Construction is underway on an expressway network. In 1980 there were 389,276 private cars registered. Because of Kuwait's small size, roadbuilding is less extensive than in Saudi Arabia, but $800 to $900 million worth of highway construction was underway in 1980.

Four major ports handle Kuwait's shipping traffic: Mina Ahmad and Mina Abdullah are primarily oil ports, the former capable of handling oil exports of up to two million barrels per day. Shuaiba and Shuwaykh are commercial ports. Shuaiba opened a container terminal in 1982 and

Shuwaykh has recently been used to handle increased exports to Iraq. Port congestion is a chronic problem; it became particularly severe in 1977, and continues to limit Kuwait's ability to absorb imports. All ports are currently under expansion. In 1980, 105.433 million metric tons were handled in Kuwaiti ports.

Kuwait has an international airport which opened in 1979 and a national airline company, Kuwait Airways Corporation.

Communications. All domestic radio and television facilities are owned and operated by the government. Kuwaiti broadcasting service operates two medium-wave transmitters and one short-wave transmitter broadcasting in Arabic and English. In 1982 there were 191,605 telephone subscriptions, 592,000 telegrams sent and 512,000 received, 8,834,000 total International Telex Communications sent and 4,801,000 outgoing telephone trunk calls made.

The Kuwaiti press is privately owned; until 1978 when strict enforcement of press restrictions imposed in 1976 began, it was considered one of the freest in the world. At present, there are only moderate restrictions on the press. It is forbidden to criticize the Emir publicly, to publish information that would undermine the national economy or currency, or to advocate the overthrow of the government by force. Nonetheless, the Kuwaiti press is not entirely government-controlled and continues to be a forum for diverse interest groups. There are five principal Arabic dailies and two English dailies: al-Anbaa (critical of government and U.S. Mideast Policy), al-Qabas (politically neutral), al-Rai al-Amm (conservative monarchist), al-Siyasa (moderate, pro-government), al-Watan (liberal, critical of government, pro-Syrian), Arab Times (liberal, popular, English language) and the Kuwait Times (middle of the road, English). Total circulation is 388,000.

12. SOCIAL SERVICES The Kuwaiti government provides its citizens with one of the most comprehensive welfare systems in the world.

Education. Education is compulsory for children between the ages of six and fourteen and is free even for many foreigners from kindergarten through university. Education is of vital importance in a country like Kuwait, where 50 percent of the population is under fifteen. School teachers include many foreigners, especially Egyptians, as well as Palestinians and Jordanians. Presently there are about 140 adult literacy centers, with an attendence of 18,000. Government efforts to stamp out illiteracy have begun to bear fruit. In 1982 the illiteracy rate among males was 28 percent and among females 46 percent. Kuwait University was founded in 1966; it has 17,000 students, 11,000 of them Kuwaitis. There are over 3,000 Kuwaitis (primarily males) studying abroad in the United States, United Kingdom, and Egypt. In 1980, the per capita spending on education was $541, representing 2.9 percent of the GNP.

Health. Health care is free for all residents; modern facilities and excellent quality of care rival conditions in some European countries. Some of the most sophisticated medical equipment in the world can be found in Kuwait, but there is a shortage of trained local personnel to operate it. In 1980, there were 257 persons for every hospital bed and 783 persons for every physician. The government is placing increasing emphasis on the production of pharmaceuticals and is providing training abroad for Kuwaiti medical and paramedical personnel to alleviate this problem. In 1982, life expectancy was 67 years for males and 72 for females.

II. POLITICAL ANALYSIS

1. SUMMARY CONCLUSIONS

1.1 RESOURCES. Oil is Kuwait's most important natural resource. Kuwait is now in the position, despite the oil glut, of having an income from oil sales and interest on investments sufficient for domestic and foreign aid needs. The oil revenues, however, have brought their own problems, including a lack of domestic investment opportunities and the collapse of the unofficial stock market. The strong entrepreneurial tradition, the insistence of the government on Kuwait's participation in any business venture, and the large volume of petrodollars have made Kuwaiti businessmen a formidable force in international markets.

1.2 SOCIAL CONFLICTS. While the government supplies a wide range of social benefits to its population of 1.6 million (both natives and foreigners), certain inequities exist. Non-Kuwaitis (who make up over 50 percent of the population) are discriminated against in housing, employment, and certain economic regulations. This discrimination is of most concern to the Palestinians, many of whom lack Kuwaiti citizenship but whose lives are bound to Kuwait. Despite lengthy residence, most Palestinians are denied naturalization into the country. The disenfranchised status of the Palestinians has led to growing bitterness and has increased the possibilities for internal disruption. Another source of friction in recent years has been increasingly fractious Sunni-Shiite relations. In addition, the crash of the Suq al-Manakh stock market revealed class and generational tensions within Kuwaiti society.

1.3 POLITICAL EVENTS. Until 1976 Kuwait was regarded as a model of enlightened Arab government. In August of that year, because of internal rivalries and dissent, Emir Sabah suspended the constitution, dissolved the National Assembly, and placed restrictions on freedom of the press.

Emir Sabah died on December 31, 1977, and was succeeded by Emir Jabir, the former prime minister and heir apparent. Subsequently, the new Emir promised elections for a new National Assembly; these were held on February 23, 1981, and produced a decidedly more conservative parliament.

1.4 SECURITY AND FOREIGN RELATIONS. As a small country with a small population, Kuwait's security depends on a judicious use of its two major resources, oil and money. In this respect, Kuwait has succeeded by taking on the role of benefactor, maintaining favorable relations with all the different camps of the Arab world, and playing an active role in the international financial community. The Iran-Iraq war has added new security strains. Kuwaiti oil installations were attacked in October 1981, contributing to the maintenance of Kuwait's production at the below-capacity level of about 800,000 barrels per day. Market conditions and a fire in mid-1981 at the Shuaiba tank farm also contributed to this level. Finally, Iranian air attacks on Kuwait-bound oil tankers in mid-1984 threatened to reduce Kuwait's oil exports and consequntly oil revenues.

1.5 INTERNAL PROBLEMS. Despite successes, Kuwait faces a number of serious problems, including Iranian-fomented subversion, increasing religious activism, the agitation of Palestinian activist groups, and the attraction of young adults to political radicalism or Islamic fundamentalism. The government's response to many of the dissident groups has been restrained (deportation rather than imprisonment or execution), thus depriving its critics of martyrs and rallying points.

1.6 EXTERNAL THREATS. For many years, disputed territorial claims between Kuwait and Iraq led to border skirmishes between the two countries; Kuwait remains in a tenuous position in relation to its more powerful neighbor. Currently over-shadowing the threat from Iraq is the challenge posed by Iran under Khomeini. Iran has not only launched several air raids on Kuwaiti territory since the begining of the Iran-Iraq war, but is also quite capable and willing to stir up trouble among the Shiite and/or religious conservatives of Kuwait.

1.7 FUTURE PROSPECTS. The Kuwaiti government will continue to face all the problems associated with rapid social and economic change. The most serious of these is the ill-will built up by resident aliens. The response of the ruling family has been deliberate and cautious. Although this policy has been successful thus far, discontent will be increasingly more difficult to contain in the future. Kuwait is equally vulnerable to external events, particularly the outcome of the Iran-Iraq war, the ongoing Arab-Israeli conflict, and Soviet machinations in the area. Because of these destabilizing forces, Kuwait will likely experience greater unrest than in previous years. The prognosis is fair to good that the regime can continue to cope with these threats.

2. POLITICAL STRUCTURE

2.1 TRADITIONAL INSTITUTIONS AND LEADERSHIP. Kuwait is basically an oligarchy made up of the old merchant families, but the effect of oil income has been to concentrate political power in the hands of the ruling Al Sabah family. Nevertheless, the traditional consultative process among the Al Sabah, leaders of the major merchant families, and the various tribes still remains a vital part of Kuwaiti politics.

Succession to the title of Emir (Ruler) is limited to the descendants of Mubarak the Great, the first Emir in the 20th century. The office has alternated between the Al Jabir and the Al Salim branches of the Al Sabah family. While this rule of alternation was disregarded in 1965, the selection of Emir Jabir (from the Al Jabir branch) in 1978 restored the balance. It has been an unwritten rule that the heir apparent also holds the position of Prime Minister. The accession of the Crown Prince and Prime Minister to the throne in 1978 set off a vigorous contest among leading members of the Al Salim branch. Eventually, a choice of successor was made in Shaikh Saad al-Abdallah Al Salim, a graduate of the Hendon Police College in England, the former Minister of Defense and the Interior.

Unlike Bahrain's House of Khalifa, Kuwait's House of Sabah maintains a low profile, rarely being seen in public. The Al Sabah share the 16-man cabinet with eleven commoners, albeit "heritage" men from the families close to them since 1710, when they all came from the desert to settle this stretch of the Gulf.

Government Structure. Kuwait is a constitutional monarchy. The judicial system, theoretically based directly on Islamic law, is in fact an adaptation of the Egyptian code. Kuwait had an elected National Assembly and a free press until August of 1976, when the Emir suspended parts of the constitution, dissolved the assembly, and clamped down on the press. Divisions in the Arab world, the turmoil in Lebanon, and the press's open criticism of Kuwait's larger neighbors were factors in this action. Conspiracy theories were widespread; it was thought that Kuwait, like Lebanon and Jordan would face civil war. Vocal opposition in the National Assembly to the government and cabinet ministers also prompted the move.

Identifiable opposition blocks within the assembly had emerged as early as 1963, demanding union with the United Arab Republic, nationalization of the Kuwaiti oil industry, and normalizing foreign policy in favor of a shift away from close ties to the west. Bedouin members of the assembly often aligned with nationalist opposition members to block the passage of government-sponsored bills, a situation that became especially pronounced in the assembly elected in 1975. While the closing of the assembly had little effect on the functioning of the oligarchical system of government, the removal of a public forum for airing grievances contributed to the increase of tension within the country. This was exacerbated by the subsequent revolution in Iran and outbreak of the Iran-Iraq war.

Recent Developments. On August 24, 1980, Emir Jabir announced that elections for a new National Assembly would be held early the following year. The elections were held on February 24, 1981. Because only male Kuwaiti citizens have the right to vote, the size of the total electorate is only about 90,000. Out of these, 41,676 Kuwaitis voted for 447 candidates for the 50 assembly seats. Charges of bribery and gerrymandering to increase the strength of the Bedouin were rife. The composition of the new assembly was far more conservative than that of its predecessors. Twenty-four members were Bedouin with a background of loyalty to the ruling family, thirteen were young technocrats, four were Islamic traditionalists, three were Arab nationalists, and only two were Shiites, although Shiite candidates had constituted more than a third of the total field. Perhaps the most surprising result was the defeat of Dr. Ahmad al-Khatib, one of the founding members of the Arab Nationalist Movement (ANM) and a leading opponent of the Al Sabah regime (he is often mistakenly considered a Marxist).

Non-Formal Institutions. Kuwait is still organized along tribal and family lines. Nightly gatherings, called diwaniyas, are the true heart of Kuwaiti society. They are a tradition dating back to when only tribes roamed Arabia and chieftains gathered their men to drink coffee and consult on everything from politics to gossip. Ordinarily an all-male event, diwaniyas begin at about 8:30

in the evening and continue until midnight. On certain nights the Emir's own diwaniya is open to anyone who wishes to come. When elections are in the offing, diwaniyas are the place for preliminary maneuvering. During political campaigns, candidates make the rounds with their promises to all the various gatherings. Since Kuwaitis enjoy great freedom of expression, the debates are often lively and the arguments long.

2.2 MILITARY, POLICE AND SECURITY. The mission of the military is purely defense-oriented. Kuwaiti military officials have acknowledged that the small military organization would be hard pressed to hold out for any long period of time against larger military organizations in the region. Their aim, in the event of attack, would be to deter attackers until an international body or group of Arab states could come to Kuwait's rescue. However, on a visit to Washington in June 1984, Kuwait's Defense Minister told Casper Weinberger, U.S. Secretary of Defense, that keeping the oil supply routes open "is our affair" and urged U.S. officials not to use American military forces in the Gulf.

Since independence, the Kuwaiti military establishment has been quite small. The 1961 Anglo-Kuwaiti treaty, which provided for British defense assistance to Kuwait, was replaced with a treaty of friendship when Britain withdrew from the Gulf in 1971. Nevertheless, British advisors and support have continued to play a key role in the formation of the modern Kuwaiti military. Kuwait received about 95 percent of its arms from Britain between 1961 and 1973.

When border problems erupted with Iraq in 1973, the government began a major expansion of the armed forces. Military spending increased from 1.5 percent of the GNP in 1974 to 4.2 percent in 1981. From 1981 to 1984, $20.2 billion was allocated for defense. Most of the expenditure has gone to the purchase of sophisticated weapons systems, many of them purchased from the United States, including the time-proved Hawk missile, the A-4 Skyhawk aircraft, and the TOW anti-tank missile. Several thousand Kuwaiti military personnel have been trained in the United States.

Kuwait's policy of keeping ties with the widest possible range of foreign sources of military assistance has led it to purchase hardware from a dozen or so countries. According to the U.S. Arms Control and Disarmament Agency, between 1978 and 1982, Kuwait purchased $150 million in arms from Great Britain, $300 million from the USA, $30 million from the USSR and $40 million from West Germany (current dollars). The emirate acquired a small quantity of SAM-7 missiles and anti-aircraft guns from the Soviet Union in 1977. In the last year it has ordered a dozen fighter-trainers from Britain and a dozen Mirage interceptors, as well as a half-dozen Super Puma helicopters (equipped with Exocet missiles) from France and armored personnel carriers from the USA. The military relies on technical expertise and training from Great Britain, the United States, Pakistan, Jordan, and Egypt, although a treaty was signed with the Soviet Union in July 1984 to provide $327 million in anti-aircraft and anti-ship missiles, in addition to military training.

There is some doubt whether this expenditure substantially increases Kuwait's military effectiveness. First, there is little logistical coordination of the disparate weapons systems. Second, all of Kuwait's military and security organizations suffer from chronic manpower problems. The army contains 10,000 troops, with 18,000 reserves. While officers tend to be drawn from well-established Kuwaiti families, trained in Britain or France, the great majority of enlisted men are more recent arrivals to Kuwait, including members of tribes that have long roamed southern Iraq and Kuwait. Their loyalty has been of some question, particularly in clashes with Iraq during the 1970s. Kuwait has instituted a draft in 1978, but a senior Kuwaiti military official has readily acknowledged the difficulties of getting young Kuwaitis from important families to enter the military and serve out their terms. The air force numbers 1,900 men, and although well-trained relies to some degree on expatriate pilots and foreign advisors. It requires assistance from the Saudi AWACS system to defend Kuwait air space effectively. The navy is small, approximately 500 men, with 58 patrol ships primarily intended as a coast guard, with little defensive capability. In spite of attractive salaries and benefits, Kuwaitis generally choose commercial and business positions rather than serving in the military. Unlike the Saudi ruling family, the military as a career ranks low in the list of choices for the Al Sabah family.

The Minister of Defense, Shaikh Salim al-Sabah al-Salim Al Sabah, (47, Oxford-educated, former ambassador to the U.S. and Canada), directs the army, the air force, and the national guard through the army chief of staff. The Minister of Interior, Shaikh Nawwaf al-Ahmad al Jabir, Al Sabah, is in charge of the public security forces, the police, and the coast guard. Most other top military posts are also held by members of the Al Sabah family.

In the event of external or internal threats to Kuwait's stability, it is critically important that the regime persuade Kuwaitis who are both competent and loyal to serve in command position in the military and security forces.

2.3 FOREIGN POLICY RESPONSIBILITIES. Fifty-five year old Shaikh Sabah al-Ahmad al-Jabir Al Sabah has been Minister of Foreign Affairs since 1963. Since 1981 he has also been Minister of Information, and since 1978 a Deputy Prime Minister, probably designating that he is next in line for the throne after Saad. Kuwait has always put its faith in pragmatism and flexibility, permanently maneuvering – never wholly Arab, never wholly Persian – among the three regional powers (Iraq, Saudi Arabia and Iran) which surround it at the head of the Gulf. Kuwait has also always pursued a more open-minded toreign policy than its neighbors and by implication shown a readiness to understand the other party's point of view.

For the time being the country's external vulnerability outweighs its internal vulnerability to Shiite subversion. Though the government is very vocal in advertising its mistrust of its Shiite population and discriminates against them in opportunities and promotions within the armed services and the administration, many politically aware Kuwaitis maintain that the Shiites, as an anxious minority, are more loyal than the Sunnis and many of them have been established in Kuwait for a good deal longer. Anti-Shiite prejudice infuriates the more open-minded Sunnis, who feel that Islamic fundamentalism, in its course, like Nasserism and secular creeds before it, and that by the example it sets at home Khomeini's revolution is losing, not gaining Kuwaiti recruits.

Their sense of external vulnerability to their regional neighbors has caused those responsible for Kuwaiti foreign policy to back away from their insistence on international non-alignment. Foreign Minister Sabah Al Sabah recently defined the Gulf as an international as well as a regional waterway. While emphasizing Kuwait does not want foreign bases on its soil in mid-June 1984, Kuwait asked the U.S. for anti-aircraft missiles, Shaikh Sabah even making an unusual public appeal to Congress. Failing to get it from the U.S., however, they turned to the USSR and closed a deal on August 14, 1984.

2.4 RELIGIOUS AFFAIRS. Until recently, confessional loyalty was not a matter of great concern to the regime. Unlike Saudi Arabia, the legitimacy of the ruling family is not primarily based on religion. Religious leaders (ulama) have had less say in policymaking, and women participate to a much greater extent in the economic life of the country than in other Gulf states. Although alcoholic beverages are illegal, they are obtainable for high prices on the black market, and officials turn a blind eye to their importation by diplomats. Kuwait has resisted Saudi pressure to close nightclubs and enforce the prohibition of alcohol as an unwarranted intrusion into internal affairs.

The Shiite minority in Kuwait, numbering 250,000, makes up 18 to 20 percent of the population. Perhaps one-quarter of these are Kuwaiti citizens, while the rest are recent or long term immigrants from Iraq, Iran, or Pakistan. Until the rise of Shiite fundamentalism stimulated by Iran, Shiites and Sunnis coexisted relatively peacefully and most still do. A number of Shiites are merchants, making up part of the Kuwaiti establishment.

2.5 POLITICAL OPPOSITION. Although political parties do not exist in Kuwait, political campaigning at election time is intense, largely through the diwaniyas. Without the focal point of the Assembly, moreover, the cohesion of such groups has diminished, except possibly for dissident groups.

In the old National Assembly, there were a number of "leftist" deputies who formed, in effect, the opposition party. Their goals and ideology, while antithetical to continued Al Sabah control of the country, could best be described as Arab nationalist or even liberal. In the new Assembly, the closest thing to an opposition group is the bloc of Sunni fundamentalists, but with only four votes, they do not constitute a parliamentary threat. The vast majority of votes in the National Assembly support the decisions of the Emir.

Expatriate Issues. The desire for Kuwaiti citizenship by Palestinians and other Arabs who regard Kuwait as a permanent home is one of the most pressing and difficult domestic problems facing the government. Many of those were homeless Palestinians who emigrated to Kuwait after 1948 (unlike other aliens who had homes elsewhere) and had no place to which they could return. Thus, they brought with them their families, settled down, and over time have risen to some of the most responsible positions in government and business. Palestinians are the predominent force in Kuwait's civil service and professions, and are absolutely unique in their role in journalism. They are very influential, but unlike the Palestinians in Lebanon they do not live in camps and are not armed. Barriers still prevent Palestinians from full social assimilation among the proud Arabian families who comprise the bulk of the "real" Kuwaiti population. However, Kuwait's immigration law does allow for the naturalization of a certain number of non-Kuwaitis every year. Naturalized Kuwaitis do not have the right to vote. Some Palestinians who have held prominent positions in Kuwait and others – often wives of Kuwaitis – have been made citizens.

The resident alien population continues to protest the slow rate of intake. The Palestinian or other foreigner who has lived in Kuwait for 20 years without citizenship has no more right to stay in Kuwait and enjoy its benefits than the most recently arrived Korean construction worker. The government can and has summarily expelled several dozen Palestinians in recent years for political activities considered to be inimical to the regime.

Palestinians in Kuwait do not hesitate, even in the presence of foreigners, to voice their complaints about what they consider discriminatory policies in employment, citizenship, and housing. Well-educated Palestinians often wax bitter about their status as employees of Kuwaitis who have only half their education and experience.

For their part, while greatly concerned about the problem, Kuwaitis generally have been unwilling to liberalize naturalization laws. Although changes made in late 1981 have made naturalization somewhat easier for residents of 20 years or more, even the most liberal, western-educated Kuwaitis believe in the policy of "Kuwait for Kuwaitis." They believe justice for the Palestinians (i.e., home, citizenship, and the right to vote) must be accomplished in Palestine rather than in Kuwait. This sentiment is underscored by Kuwait's very vocal pro-Palestinian foreign policy.

Palestinian Residents. Kuwait is a major PLO center, one in which the mainstream factions supporting Arafat predominate. (In fact, Arafat lived in Kuwait before establishing al-Fatah in 1964). Kuwait's government supports the PLO financially (less the more radical factions), but makes sure that Palestinian activities are limited to fund raising. If Palestinians do not avoid domestic politics, they are quickly expelled. To keep the Palestinians in line, the regime threatens cancellation of their many benefits if they do not police themselves.

In this way the regime induces the entire Palestinian community to deal with potential trouble-makers. Indeed, the government closely watches all foreign residents and periodically expels those without legal status to reduce the prospect of internal unrest and to remind the non-Kuwaiti communities that their position in the country is tenuous and revocable. In November 1982, over 25,000 persons were declared illegal aliens and ordered to leave.

2.6 ROLE OF THE ECONOMY. After the 1973 oil embargo and increase in oil prices when Kuwait began to accumulate large cash surpluses, the former Minister of Finance and Oil Abd al-Rahman Salem al-Atiqi (now Kuwait's representative to the Islamic Development Bank and Financial Advisor to the Emir) occasionally told visitors, "Kuwait is a poor country, all we have is money." The statement rarely failed to produce the intended laughter – not difficult since the audiences were usually composed of bankers, entrepreneurs, or finance ministers of developing countries, all asking the minister to fulfill some financial request.

Minister al-Atiqi, however, intended this remark as a serious comment on the doubts which he shared with others (of the pre-wealth generation of Kuwaitis) about the benefits of the immense wealth the country enjoyed. This wealth has brought Kuwait serious social problems.

Growth and Development. The mid-1970s was a time of high income and high spending. Although revenues continued to rise in the latter part of the 1970s, government spending slowed markedly. This cooling off reflected the completion or near completion of many major infrastructure projects in Kuwait's long-term development plan. It also reflected a desire to check spiraling inflation, caused by an overheated economy, as well as Kuwait's more sensible and businesslike approach to development in comparison to other countries in the region. The Kuwaitis watched other Gulf states rush into petrochemical projects with no heed given to the implications of several projects coming on stream simultaneously. There is still a dearth of regional economic planning or coordination in the Gulf, but the Gulf Cooperation Council has since 1981 begun to make progress on this front.

Senior officials in finance and planning positions in the government and in the Industrial Bank of Kuwait, a major planning and development organization for non-petroleum projects, have advocated a policy of restrained growth which funds practical and commercially sound projects. However, the powerful merchant families of Kuwait have always labored against this policy, pushing for as many major development projects as quickly as possible, because more construction means better sales and more commissions benefiting these same Kuwaiti merchants. Thus, there is a continuing competition for royal favor among those wanting more spending and those who counsel restraint. Generally, the latter prevail.

Kuwait's size has also restrained growth, since the small population and relatively small land area require much less infrastructure than Saudi Arabia, for example. Further, the absence of raw materials other than hydrocarbons and a lack of skilled labor limit Kuwait's development. There are limits to what even those who favor more spending could reasonably propose.

Kuwaiti Assets. The 1983-84 Kuwaiti budget was $12.1 billion. Even with oil production at around half the preferred level (and well below the allotted OPEC quota), oil earnings essentially continue to cover financial requirements. Until recently, annual income levels and the country's limited absorptive capacity meant that large surpluses were inevitable; these have been translated into holdings of foreign assets which further contribute to revenue. For the first time in 1982, income from foreign assets exceeded oil earnings. Much of Kuwait's surplus is accumulated in Kuwait's foreign reserve holdings. For example, the Kuwait Fund for Future Generations receives by law 10 percent of all government oil revenues. The Fund is for use in the distant days when Kuwait's oil reserves are depleted. The official foreign reserves are estimated at $72 billion.

The oil glut and the OPEC price cut have slowed the accumulation of surplus funds. However, it has not been necessary to draw down foreign reserve holdings. The reserve funds and Kuwait's portfolio of foreign investments will almost certainly continue to grow. Kuwait will continue to be a net exporter of capital.

Kuwait has moved to develop overseas assets which will deepen and strengthen its economic position. It has acquired major producing and downstream entities overseas, beginning in 1981 with the U.S. firm of Santa Fe International, a multinational drilling and exploration company. In early 1984, Kuwait agreed to buy Gulf Oil Corporation's Italian refining and oil marketing operations, doubling Kuwaiti-owned gasoline stations in Europe to nearly 3,000. These moves are aimed at ensuring marketing facilities for refined petroleum products during the glut, which has severely reduced crude oil sales. Kuwait thereby improves prospects for competitive marketing of its own refined products.

The Merchant State. In addition to oil and financial assets, the government controls most large industry through public corporations. Yet despite the dominance of the public sector in the economy, Kuwait is a merchant state with a long and strong entrepreneurial tradition. Business law in Kuwait reinforces this tradition. The participation of a Kuwaiti citizen is required for almost every type of business activity; a Kuwaiti or Kuwaiti entity must hold at least 51 percent ownership in any foreign business venture; Kuwaiti agents are required on most purchasing contracts; only Kuwaitis can speculate in the local stock market or own land; imports must be in the name of registered Kuwaiti importers; and the government makes a strenuous effort to see that Kuwaiti contractors are involved in government projects.

These circumstances make every Kuwaiti literally a born businessman. Estimated per capita GDP stands at over $16,000, but this figure greatly underestimates the welfare of most Kuwaitis. For example, because Kuwait imports almost all its needed goods and services, and because Kuwaiti participation is required in these transactions, a Kuwaiti with limited or no background at all in business need only find a capable business manager (Palestinian, Egyptian, British, American, etc.) in order to produce a substantial income. He can also obtain long-term no-interest loans to build his house, get free professional advice and research information if he contemplates going into a new business, and receive government subsidies for start-up and manufacturing costs. If his business ventures go awry, he can ask the government for help – with a good chance of getting it. For example, in 1978, tight credit conditions in Kuwait produced sudden losses for Kuwaitis involved in the local stock market; the government paid out more than $600 million to save the speculators. However, the crash of the unofficial stock market in August-September 1982, involving financial losses of as much as $90 billion, has created deep concern without final agreement on how much investors should be bailed out.

The old-line merchant families still have the lion's share of profit from these merchant activities. While many younger members of these families and other less "established" Kuwaitis are also competing for and winning significant shares of business, there is still resentment on the part of many outside the establishment.

Kuwait's tradition of trading and the experience of some of the merchant families in business in the Far East, the subcontinent, and throughout the Arab world, have made Kuwaitis formidable businessmen outside their own country. Their aggressive business instincts are known, if not appreciated, throughout the Middle East. Two of the major merchant dynasties in Kuwait today are the families of al-Ghanim and Alireza. They come from vastly different backgrounds and operate with vastly different styles, the former coming from the desert in 1710 and close – socially and politically – to the Al Sabahs, while the latter is of Persian origin (via Bahrain and Saudi Arabia) and newly arrived as of 1949 in Kuwait.

A word should be said for the Kuwaiti businesswomen. Kuwaiti women enjoy a great deal of freedom, and many of them operate successful businesses, including construction, currency trading and investment, importing, and retailing. Despite advances, only 2.5% of Kuwaiti women are actually active in the labor force.

The Welfare State. The Kuwaiti welfare state dates from the time of its independence. In 1962, the Public Assistance Law provided for public assistance to widows, orphans, the disabled and sick, and low-income families. Food, largely imported, is heavily subsidized. Medical benefits within the emirate are free to both citizens and non-citizens. The education system is also highly developed, and free from the primary up to the university level. The number of students at each level has expanded considerably since 1970. Primary and secondary school enrollment have each doubled, to 125,000 and 150,000 respectively. Female enrollment has increased to the point that it approaches male enrollment, except at the university and vocational levels. Of the student population 40 to 55 percent are non-Kuwaiti citizens.

There are political ramifications to the expansion of the welfare state for both Kuwaitis and non-Kuwaitis. The benefits are not uniformly distributed. In the area of housing, there is clear discrimination against non-Kuwaitis. In the field of education, only Kuwaiti males are sent abraod for university and post graduate work. Interestingly, both women and non-Kuwaitis enrolled at the University of Kuwait have a higher ratio of completion than men, perhaps because they see education as a way of improving their status. Kuwaiti men, on the other hand, have little incentive to finish an educational program leading to gainful employment. Because investment opportunities are readily available to them, they are not motivated to pursue the vocational and technical education necessary for the future development of Kuwait; similarly, they are unwilling to involve themselves in manual labor. Consequently, Kuwait will remain an importer of foreign labor as long as the present system exists.

The economic ramifications of the social welfare system are also beginning to surface. It is increasingly costly to administer. Until his resignation as Finance and Planning Minister last year, Abd al-Latif al-Hamad, father of the Kuwait Development Fund, advocated "rationalizaion" of social services. This entailed reducing the number of benefits available to those Kuwaitis who could afford to pay for them. Needless to say, this was unpopular with the Kuwaiti population. A similar reduction for non-Kuwait citizens would provoke considerable unrest and is politically unfeasible.

Housing. To relieve a critical housing shortage, Kuwait is allocating about $1 billion a year for new housing and related development. The program for public housing, however, could create problems because Kuwaiti nationals get a clear preference over non-Kuwaitis in terms of mortgages, interest rates and availability and quality of housing. Furthermore, the non-Kuwaiti, because he cannot own land in Kuwait, is at the mercy of Kuwaiti landlords when it comes to rent. In building Kuwaiti-only housing projects, the government is creating a highly visible and easily understood symbol of the difference between those who have and those who "have-not-as-much."

Employment. Employment is a another potential point of conflict between the Kuwaiti government and its non-Kuwaiti population. All Kuwaitis are guaranteed jobs; of late, Kuwaitis are guaranteed higher salaries than their non-Kuwaiti counterparts, even though the work is the same. One can, for example, see the non-Kuwaiti manager of a branch bank drive home in his aging Fiat, while the Kuwaiti cashier, who earns three times the salary for less work, roars away in a new Mercedes. The problem is most acute for Palestinians, the majority of whom do not have Kuwaiti citizenship but whose lives are bound to the country. There are Palestinians who have worked in Kuwait for more than 30 years, and there are many young Palestinians who were born in Kuwait. The experienced Palestinian engineer, teacher or government worker must yield preference in both salary and status to the recently returned Kuwaiti graduate. This is a political as well as economic issue, since Kuwait supports the eventual return of Palestinians to their own land.

Among the transient workers (who intend to work in Kuwait for a short period of time), there is less resentment toward native Kuwaitis, since they would not be in Kuwait if they weren't earning substantially more than they could earn at home.

In the spring of 1984, Kuwait issued strict new rules governing work permits for expatriates employed in the private sector, in an effort to rationalize and regulate foreign workers. This is also a security measure in light of the spate of bombings there in December 1983.

The measures followed a Gulf labor symposium held in Kuwait in April of 1984 where various Gulf labor experts assessed the labor problems and needs of the region and recommended that labor be recruited within the framework of the economic and social development of the region and the strict control of the flow of foreign labor to the Gulf.

Among the foreign work force, after the Arab component, the Pakistanis and Indians are the most entrenched. An increasing number of East Asians have joined the foreign work force.

2.7 FACTORS FOR STABILITY AND INSTABILITY. For all its vocalizing in support of Arab nationalist positions, the native Kuwaiti population has always been conservative, particularly in comparison to the disenfranchised (but thoroughly bourgeois) resident Palestinian community. Nevertheless, the conservative mandate of the new Assembly is surprising. At best, it could be seen as a stabilizing domestic trend. On the other hand, militant Sunni conservatism could be as destabilizing as radicalism from the other end of the political spectrum. The appearance of Sunni fundamentalists in the Assembly is a somewhat disturbing indication of an overall shift to the right. One indication of this shift was the 1982 rejection of female suffrage, with many liberal members abstaining; another was the passage of a law in 1983 denying citizenship to non-Muslims. Such a legislative trend could result in the deterioration of relations with the disenfranchised elements, particularly the Palestinians, and an increase of confessional tension between Sunnis and Shiites. The government appears capable of managing such strains in the near future provided external threats do not become realities.

3.
RECENT DEVELOPMENTS AND THE PROBLEMS OF STABILITY

3.1 POLITICAL STRATEGY. Running through all of Kuwait's politics, both foreign and domestic, is the realization that Kuwait has but two major resources, oil and money. A small country with a small population, a minority of which is actually Kuwaiti, the country has little else to protect it from enemies at home or abroad. Thus, the Kuwaiti regime has attempted to make itself "the goose that lays the golden eggs." Abroad, it has attempted to bestow its largess in such a manner as to gain political and military support from other countries in exchange for economic assistance. At home, its cradle-to-grave welfare system leaves little for dissidents to demand. Even Palestinians, who receive second-class treatment, have too much at stake to risk throwing it away. By following these policies Kuwait has managed to take a strong and often radical stand on issues such as oil prices, the Arab-Israeli question, and the Palestinian issue without risking its security. However, Kuwait almost never acts until it feels there is a solid consensus in the Arab world, in OPEC, or at home.

3.2 SOCIOECONOMIC PROBLEMS. Signs of increasing social malaise suggest an issue which could strengthen the hand of Islamic militants. While traditional values rooted in family and religion have provided stability and continuity for Kuwait's society, easily acquired affluence, along with a lack of meaningful challenges to absorb intellectual energies have introduced problems which Arab societies have traditionally not experienced. In 1981, the social implications of cases of kidnapping, rape, armed robbery and murder were dismissed because the perpetrators were foreigners. In 1982 a kidnapping committed by the son of a well-to-do Kuwaiti businessman shattered such complacency. The young man's reported drug addiction pointed to another development of recent years.

The Suq al-Manakh Stock Market Crash. The crash of the Suq al-Manakh market occurred in August-September 1982. Although an official stock exchange (the eighth largest in the world) has existed since 1977, a parallel stock market soon arose because of the stringent requirements placed on the official market. It deals in the shares of Gulf companies based in Bahrain and the UAE, with largely Kuwaiti ownership and management. Due to rapid increase in national income and consumer savings, demand exceeded the supply of the number of shares available for trading, and there was a large degree of speculation during 1981 and the first quarter of 1982. While the Kuwaiti government officials foresaw the economic dangers of an unofficial, unregulated market, the al-Manakh market (presently back in business) played a valuable social role. It made possible the transfer of substantial wealth to the ambitious – and potentially volatile – lower and middle classes, many of whose members made fortunes from speculation. The crash occurred because of the increased use of deferred payment deals – buying shares with post-dated checks. In addition to speculators, there was a small number of dishonest investors who set up fictitious corporations and purchased stock with bad checks. There were some rumors that high-ranking government officials were among this group. To check the panic and keep the damage to the Kuwaiti economy to a minimum, the government intervened in September, 1982. A law intended to regulate the use of post-dated payment was passed.

The Suq al-Manakh crash was more than a financial crisis. It has undermined the essential trust and confidence which formerly underlay transactions in Kuwait and it has brought to the surface latent hostilities between the favored old ruling families and the new class of educated young men who have just recently acquired their wealth. New frustrations and feelings of alienation are evident and pose a problem for the regime that must be resolved.

3.3 POLITICAL OPPOSITION. Among the disaffected young adults of Kuwait, those who are not attracted to Islamic fundamentalism as a means of expressing dissatisfaction turn to secular political radicalism. The paucity of outlets for political expression has caused dissenters to move underground. Small groups of young political leftists are reportedly meeting clandestinely in Kuwait, and both leftist and Islamic sentiment is growing stronger at the Kuwait University campus. Professional groups –

doctors, engineers, architects – are also the focus for political discussion and verbal dissent. These organizations are generally dominated by non-Kuwaitis.

The Government's response to active dissidents, whether religious or political, remains restrained. The standard procedure for punishing dissidents has been to deport them as quickly as possible. The execution of the Islamic Jihad members in March 1984 was a case of the authorities' use of stronger measures.

The Sunni Right. The strengthening of religious activism in Kuwait has two aspects: 1) a desire by many Sunnis to reinstate the traditional values of Islam, which, they believe, have been weakened by commercialism and westernization; and 2) Shiite militancy inspired by the revolution in Iran.

Sunni dissatisfaction is less well defined than Shiite activism, but it cuts across economic and age groups. There are a number of young, well-educated Westernized Kuwaitis who, disillusioned with the blandishments of western culture, have become adherents of very conservative religious views and subscribe to Muslim Brotherhood doctrine. This phenomenon is happening not only in Kuwait but all over the Islamic world. Fundamentalist Islamic groups reject the pragmatism and com promises of the religious establishment of Sunni Islam, which has historically been more quiescent and supportive of the political status quo than has Shia Islam. Movements such as the Muslim Brotherhood have had less strength in Kuwait than elsewhere because the Kuwaiti government, through its generous social welfare programs and relative lack of corruption, has not allowed specific issues to develop which could become rallying cries for the disaffected. Nevertheless, there has risen a Sunni fundamentalist bloc in the National Assembly, and two ministers thought to be members of the local Muslim Brothers group were dropped from the cabinet in 1981. Government support for Islam is strong, and the Al Sabah family maintains lines of communication with every significant religious group in Kuwaiti society. Under the influence of the religious right, the government has noticeably curbed the liberal atmosphere of the 1970s by restricting co-education to the university level and by banning the importation of liquor, even to diplomatic posts.

The Shiites. There are 250,000 Shiites in Kuwait, one quarter of them native to the country, while the rest are resident aliens or immigrant workers. Although few Shiites have held high government positions (there is only one Shiite cabinet minister and only two in the National Assembly), there are a number of powerful Shiite merchants whose families originally came from Iraq, Iran, and Saudi Arabia. Because Al Sabah leadership has always sought the counsel of the merchants, this element of the Shiite community has had access to the political establishment.

In Kuwait the consequence of the Iranian revolution has been agitation by local Shiite militants, intrigues sponsored by the Iranian government, and increased vigilence by Kuwaiti Sunnis. There have been several instances of Shiite activism in the last two years, including a large demonstration near the U.S. embassy, the distribution of leaflets, the semi-clandestine circulation of cassette tapes with political messages, and calls for a return to Islamic law. At the same time, high-ranking Shiite government officials have been accused of corruption, several Kuwait University officials were dismissed for "administrative irregularities," and several Shiites have been expelled for activities deemed harmtul to Kuwaiti interests. The Shiite community has alleged that Shiites are being edged out of the army and police and a Sunni mob recently burned a Shiite mosque. Several Shiite mosques were torn down in th name of urban revewal and were replaced by Sunni mosques. While a serious confessional rift does not seem imminent, tensions remain high.

The December 1983 Bombings. Kuwaiti authorities had managed to capture several groups of infiltrators between 1980 and 1983, but the impossibility of securing both land and sea frontiers meant they could not be 100 percent successful. On December 12, 1983, well-coordinated car-bomb attacks were carried out on seven targets in Kuwait, including the US and French embassies, American commercial concerns, and Kuwait government installations. Six people were killed and eighty-six injured in the 90-minute spate of bombings.

Twenty-five men were put on trial for the crime and, in March 1984, six men were sentenced to death and most of the others to varying terms of imprisonment. Most of the terrorists were Iraqi Shiites apparently financed by and operating from Iran. Several Kuwaiti Shiites were also involved, as were two Lebanese Shiites (who were reputed to have links with Husain Musawi's Islamic Amal group in Lebanon's Bekaa Valley) and one Lebanese Christian. As a consequence of the bombings, visa requirements were tightened, and plans were made to strengthen the coast guard to prevent infiltration by sea.

The Secular Opposition. Almost from its beginning, Kuwait's National Assembly has served as a prominent forum for secular liberal opposition to the government. Although never formally organized as a political party (political organizations are illegal in Kuwait), liberal-Arab nationalist groupings have long published election manifestos and been represented in the press by the weekly newspaper al-Talia. The most prominent spokesmen for this point of view have been Dr. Ahmad al-Khatib, one of the founders of the now-fragmented Arab Nationalists Movement, and former Kuwait University professor Abdullah al-Nafisi. Liberal goals have focused on strict adherence to the Kuwaiti constitution in reducing the power of the ruling family and in the strengthening of democracy through electoral reform and a broader role for the National Assembly, as well as calling for a diversified (capitalist) economy, liberalized naturalization laws, and progress toward Arab unity.

While the liberal-Arab nationalist bloc had been present in nearly all the elected National Assemblies, it was particularly vociferous in the 1975 Assembly in denouncing the class structure of Kuwaiti society and demanding nationalization of the oil company and strict measures in the conservation of oil resources. The alliance of this group with Bedouin members in obstructing government-sponsored legislation provoked the regime to suspend the Assembly in August 1976. Almost all of the Liberal candidates were defeated in the 1981 elections for a new Assembly. While concern has been focused in recent years on the strength of the Islamic right, it cannot be assumed that the relatively moderate liberal opposition, though fragmented, has disappeared or will remain moderate.

Military Dissidence. There have been few indications of discontent in the Kuwaiti military or security forces, although dissidence was reported at the Infantry College in 1979. The fact that the Kuwaiti armed forces have one clearly defined potential enemy (Iraq) is presumably the main reason for their loyalty. There is no evidence of unrest within their ranks or of any anti-government conspiracies. In fact, it would be against all their interests to conspire against the present regime because its breakdown would inevitably mean a new bid for possession by Iraq. Nor would it be to the advantage of the Kuwaiti professional soldier (most of whom are of Kuwaiti Bedouin stock) to be overrun by the Iraqi army and incorporated into it on conditions much less attractive than those prevailing at present in Kuwait.

3.4 REGIONAL AFFAIRS: THE GULF. In February 1981, the Kuwaitis took initiatives to create the Gulf Cooperation Council. In keeping with Kuwait's overall policy aims, this move was an attempt to proceed on Gulf matters under the protective umbrella of Gulf consensus. Even then, the Kuwaitis stressed economic and cultural cooperation. It was not until August 1981, when Libya's Colonel Qaddafi signed a treaty with South Yemen and Ethiopia and followed up with a visit to the Gulf, that Kuwait agreed to concentrate more on security matters. The sense of urgency was underscored on October 1 of the same year, when Iran bombed Kuwaiti oil installations in retaliation for Kuwaiti support of the Iraqi war effort against Iran.

Since then Kuwait has participated in GCC discussion of common defense concerns. In October 1983, it took part in exercises of the GCC's rapid deployment force in the UAE. One month later, Kuwait and Saudi Arabia held joint air exercises with Kuwaiti Skyhawks and Saudi F-5s and F-15s. These first steps toward GCC military cooperation were more a political assertion of the intent of the Gulf Arab states to look after their own security than a demonstration of their capacity to do so. However, Kuwait's pronounced neutralism – evident in its strong opposition to Oman's close security relations with the US and its lobbying of GCC partners to join Kuwait in establishing diplomatic relations with the USSR and east bloc nations – has largely prevented serious progress toward a credible cooperative defense system. A coordinated GCC air defense system with command, control and communications elements has not been developed because of their differences in political and security policy. The Saudis have favored adoption of a common U.S.-manufactured fighter plane for the GCC inventory.

Gulf Security. The December 1981 coup attempt by Iranian trained and assisted Shiite dissidents in Bahrain generated deep concern for internal security in all the GCC countries. The Saudis signed bilateral pacts with Bahrain, Qatar, the UAE and Oman, and called for a multilateral treaty to promote closer cooperation against subversive threats. Kuwait, unwilling to adopt less progressive terms on extradition than its own laws require, rejected the draft multilateral treaty and refused to sign a bilateral treaty with Saudi Arabia. Recently the Kuwaitis have signalled a desire to find acceptable compromise language for a multilateral pact.

Kuwait's vulnerability to terrorism was underscored by attacks on its overseas diplomatic personnel and bombings in Kuwait itself. Kuwaiti officials in Spain and

Pakistan, the former fatally, were shot in September 1982, at the hands of a Palestinian. In December 1983, in a manner reminiscent of the earlier Beirut bombings of the US Embassy and the French and American MNF forces, terrorist bombing attacks were carried out against seven targets in Kuwait, apparently with Iranian backing. Faced with the challenge of containing Iranian-inspired subversion, the Kuwaitis are taking a tough line, adding the penalty of amputation to that of hanging according to the degree of such crimes.

Economic and Social Integration of the Gulf. In the context of the GCC, Kuwait has promoted modest movement toward economic cooperation. Thus far this has consisted mostly of the adoption of a common external tariff and alignment of other economic policies. There has been progress on limited measures such as provision for property ownership by nationals of any GCC country in any other member state, facilitation of the movement of goods between GCC states, and reduction of duplicate development schemes. A basis for future meaningful steps toward economic integration has been provided.

Kuwait is an active participant in many dialogues and conferences that are convened around the world. The operations and programs of Kuwaiti institutions such as the Institute for Scientific Research and the Industrial Bank, have been studied and emulated by neighboring states. Under the activist leadership of Oil and Finance Minister Shaikh Ali al-Khalifa Al Sabah, Kuwait has increased its influence within OPEC and OAPEC.

3.5 RELATIONS WITH SAUDI ARABIA. Ties between Kuwait and Saudi Arabia have been strong since the Al Saud sought refuge in Kuwait at the end of the 19th century; it was from Kuwait that future Saudi king Abd al-Aziz ("Ibn Saud") launched his successful recapture of Riyadh. Due to tribal protocol in the peninsula, Kuwait has at least a semblance of equality with Saudi Arabia. When the Saudi ruling family makes its annual move to its eastern palace all of the Gulf shaikhs visit except the ruler of Kuwait, who is viewed as an equal. Nonetheless, Kuwait has often had cause to be wary of the shadow of its larger neighbor. While the onshore territory of the former Neutral Zone between the two countries was amicably divided, a dispute in the late 1970s over several small islands in the Gulf apparently ended with an armed Saudi occupation of the islands. Riyadh has also placed considerable pressure on the Al Sabah to crack down on the liberal atmosphere in Kuwait, including the black market sale of alcohol and proliferation of nightclubs. Kuwaiti resentment of Saudi pressure and suspicion of Riyadh's intentions led to its refusal to sign a bilateral security agreement – the only state in the GCC to refuse – in the wake of the discovery of the 1981 coup attempt in Bahrain.

3.6 THE THREAT OF IRAQ. For most of the years since Kuwait's independence in 1961, Iraq has been considered the major threat to Kuwait. From the outset, Iraq claimed all of Kuwait as part of the old Ottoman Sanjaq of Basra. While these claims are no longer advanced, Iraq's desire for secure access to its naval base at Umm Qasr has caused it to claim a large part of Kuwait's northern border, particularly Bubayan and Warbah Islands and areas adjacent to the mainland. Iraqi bluster has from time to time turned into military maneuvers near or in Kuwait's territory, and a few Kuwaiti soldiers have been killed.

The Iraqi threat is, temporarily at least, in abeyance. Kuwait has been a major conduit of money, supplies and material for the Iraqi war effort against Iran since war broke out in September 1980. The Iraqis appear genuinely appreciative of this effort, particularly since it involves considerable risk, exemplified by the Iranian bombing of Kuwaiti oil installations in October 1981. Under pressure from its parliament, Kuwait has halted outright grants and loans to Iraq, though it has continued to provide crude oil to Iraqi customers with the revenues going to Iraq. Recent Iraqi actions to escalate the conflict in the Gulf in large measure reflect an attempt to lever more financial support from Kuwait and the other Gulf Arab states.

3.7 THE IRANIAN THREAT. Because of its ability to stir up trouble among Shiites and religious conservatives, Iran under Khomeini presents a continuing destabilizing threat. In addition, there are a number of Kuwaitis of Iranian origin and several thousand Iranian workers in Kuwait. Iran has attempted on more than one occasion to foment political agitation in Kuwait and carry out guerrilla activities. Former Iranian foreign minister Sadeq Gotbzadeh was attacked in Kuwait in April 1980, and a few days later a Kuwaiti diplomat was shot and wounded in Tehran. Shortly thereafter, two bombs exploded in front of the Iranian airlines office in Kuwait, and another bomb damaged the Iranian embassy. Iranian sabotage was suspected in July when Kuwait's electricity supply was cut, resulting in a three-day blackout. Subsequently, Iran took more direct measures in an attempt to reduce Kuwaiti support for Iraq: air attacks were made on Kuwaiti border posts in November 1980 and June 1981, and an oil installation north of Kuwait City was set ablaze by another Iranian airstrike in October 1981. The most recent Iranian threat to Kuwait came in the early summer of 1984, when Iranian jets carried out a series of attacks on oil tankers bound for Kuwait and Saudi Arabia.

Kuwait, the UAE and Saudi Arabia have spearheaded GCC efforts to mediate the Iran-Iraq war. While these, like all other mediation efforts, have not yet shown much success, it is possible that an approach involving a pledge of Arab money for repair of war damage in Iran might succeed.

3.8 REGIONAL AFFAIRS: OTHER ARAB STATES. Kuwait's regional foreign relations have been on the whole successful. Traditionally, Kuwait has always preferred a strong Egypt in the Arab world as a counterpart to Saudi Arabia, Iran, and Iraq, and has supported Saudi Arabia's lead in bringing Egypt back into the Islamic Conference.

There are two ways in which Kuwait has used its revenue surplus as an extension of its foreign policy: bilaterally and through development assistance for specific projects. After the 1973 war, Kuwait and other oil states gave bilateral aid to Egypt and Syria, the two "Steadfastness and Confrontation Front" states, to rebuild their economies. Egyptian aid was cut following Camp David, while Kuwait reduced assistance to Syria in 1982 in objection to its support of Iran.

Kuwait's assistance to Jordan, particularly after 1967, has been of considerable importance in rebuilding the Jordanian economy. In 1981 KD 21 million ($74.6 million) were granted in loans for irrigation, hydroelectric, and water supply projects. King Hussein of Jordan visited Kuwait during the first week of June 1984, offering military aid in case of attack and expecting cutbacks in Kuwait's aid to Jordan to be alleviated. Kuwaiti economic inducements have also been offered to impoverished South Yemen, to counterbalance its dependence on the Soviet Union, encouraging it to adopt a less radical stance in domestic and foreign policy. The Kuwait Fund has long been active in both Yemens in building schools, hospitals, and other development projects. Extensive aid has been given to the PLO and the Palestinian refugees through UNWRA.

Kuwait played a mediating role in ending the 1979 border war between North and South Yemen. Then, in 1983, along with the UAE, Kuwait brought to a successful conclusion diplomatic efforts to establish relations between South Yemen and Oman, ending their longstanding hostility over Aden's support of the Marxist rebellion in Oman's southern province of Dhufar. In promoting this settlement, Kuwait clearly hopes to remove part of Oman's rationale for a closer security relationship with the U.S.

At the UN Kuwait has just completed a term on the Security Council, where its ambassador served effectively and forcefully.

The Palestinians. Many observers of Kuwait have held to the simple rule that Kuwaiti support for the Palestinian cause was used to buy off the threat of Palestinian activity against the regime. While a valid consideration, this perception denigrates the genuine sympathy many Kuwaitis have for Palestinian aspirations. Most of Kuwait's support goes to Fatah, and Yasser Arafat has always maintained close ties with the Kuwaiti government. In return for this support, Fatah assists the Kuwaitis in keeping the more extreme Palestinian groups under control.

The relative freedom in Kuwait and the relatively benign attitude of the authorities toward radicals has resulted in Kuwait's being used by several activist groups. There have been bombings and incidents of violence in Kuwait, including the killing of several individuals in a PLO attack on a Kuwaiti newspaper office; the city was for a time one of the minor battlefields in the war between Iraqi intelligence and the PLO.

Kuwait's current problem is that, having allowed some of these groups to operate, it is difficult to close them down and to prevent their influence from spreading to Kuwaiti youth. Moreover, by separating their support for the Palestinian cause from their failure to redress local Palestinian grievances, most notably citizenship, Kuwait runs the risk that the two issues will not remain isolated from each other.

Settlement of the Arab-Israeli Situation. Kuwait does not see a major role for itself in any Arab-Israeli peace negotiations, but it could play a major role in financing post-settlement development projects. To reduce the perceived Palestinian threat to the regime Kuwait would support the resettlement of Palestinians in a Palestinian homeland and provide economic aid to such an entity. Until a settlement is reached, however, Kuwaitis fear that another regional blowup, war, or an even less traumatic incident could lead to an oil embargo or other disruption of supply and a subsequent U.S. military attack.

3.9 RELATIONS WITH THE UNITED STATES. The Arabian Mission Hospital of the Reformed Church of America brought medical care to Kuwait in 1909 and helped create a positive image of Americans there. Diplomatic relations were established soon after Kuwait's independence in 1961, and U.S. contacts with Kuwait on military matters began in 1971. Since then the Kuwaitis have purchased a considerable amount of American arms, including jeeps, light trucks, Hawk missiles, TOW anti-tank missiles, Sidewinder missiles, and aircraft.

Political relations between the two countries, however, have become somewhat strained in recent years. The U.S. government and American corporations suffered regular criticism in the National Assembly between the 1960s and 1976. The Israeli invasion of Lebanon and widespread Arab belief of American collaboration helped to stoke anti-American feeling and soured the American-Kuwaiti relationship, already uncomfortable to the U.S. because of Kuwait's non-alignment policy. A counselor at the U.S. embassy in Kuwait was ordered to leave the country in July 1981 and in August 1983 the Kuwaiti government refused to accept Brandon W. Grove, Jr., as the U.S. Ambassador on the official grounds that his credentials were not acceptable. The actual cause seems to have been objection to his holding the position of U.S. Consul-General in Jerusalem, which Kuwait considered illegitimate and counter to Arab claims on Jerusalem. The Kuwaiti refusal may have provoked the U.S. government refusal to sell Stinger missiles to Kuwait in May 1984, soon after a number of Stingers were sold to Saudi Arabia for defense against Iranian attacks on Kuwaiti and Saudi shipping. "When things go really bad, Kuwait will have to go by what Saudi Arabia says, and the Saudis will choose the Americans," said Asad Abd al-Rahman, a professor of political science at Kuwait University. Adds Kuwaiti parliamentarian Khalid Sultan, "We can buy weapons from any direction, but we will never permit troops."

There is one aspect of U.S.-Kuwaiti relations which warrants further attention. During the past decade increased demand has made Kuwait more dependent on the U.S. for imported food. This could make the country vulnerable to a food boycott instigated by the U.S., although such a boycott is unlikely.

3.10 RELATIONS WITH THE SOVIET BLOC. Kuwait is the only GCC state to have diplomatic relations with and to purchase arms from the Soviet Union. In addition to Soviet arms purchases, Yugoslavia has been involved in Kuwaiti military construction, and Rumania and other East European countries have assisted in Kuwaiti development projects. However, these contacts should be seen as a measure of the emirate's emphasis on a policy of nonalignment and international neutrality, rather than any ideological affinity. At the same time, Kuwait remains far more closely tied to the west than to the east. Kuwait's posture vis-a-vis the Soviet Union and the United States reflects both the broad range of public opinion there and an appreciation of its sensitive political role in the Gulf. This is most clearly seen in the $327 million arms and military training agreement announced between Kuwait and the Soviet Union. At one level, the arms deal indicates Kuwait's pragmatism in seeking its defense means from whomever it must; but it also reflects Kuwaiti as well as Saudi desires to signal Washington that there is a growing weariness with American arms policy – a policy continously marked by hesitency in supplying arms to America's Arab allies. It is noteworthy that immediately following the Kuwaiti-Soviet arms deal, the United States signed a $78 million fighter training program agreement with Kuwait that included measures for upgrading Kuwait's Hawk anti-aircraft missiles.

3.11 ECONOMIC AID AND THE THIRD WORLD. Development assistance is disbursed by Kuwait's Fund for Arab Economic Development, the oldest and most active of the Arab aid institutions, established in 1961, and the Kuwait-based Arab Fund for Economic and Social Development. The amount dispensed from January 1962 to June 1982 totalled KD 992 million ($3.436 billion [1982 dollars]). Kuwaiti aid measures from 3 to 10 percent of the country's gross national product; in 1980 it totalled 3.88 percent of the GNP. Fifty-seven percent of this aid has gone to Arab countries, 17.8 percent to African countries, and 24.9 percent to Asian countries. It should be noted that among recipient countries of aid from KFAED is the People's Republic of China.

3.12 THE SEARCH FOR ALLIES. With no credible military deterrent against external threats, Kuwait must, as always, look for allied support. The problem is that several of its potential allies, e.g., Egypt and Iran, have fallen by the wayside and others, e.g., Saudi Arabia, have no credible deterrent either. Iraq is of only limited value against Iran, bogged down as it is in the Iraq-Iran war. Syria is politically unacceptable as an ally, because of its support of Iran, resulting in Kuwait's termination of the $48 million contribution it had been making to Syrian peacekeeping forces in Lebanon. That leaves the Jordanians, and Kuwait is not at all sure it wishes to call on them or that they could provide the necessary miltary support or stem a fait accompli. Thus, the Kuwaitis have few alternatives in case of a military attack and all the more reason look to the strengthening of the GCC to fill this need.

4. FUTURE PROSPECTS

4.1 INTERNAL UNREST. There are real and potentially serious threats to the stability of the current government in Kuwait. The generous application of petrodollars has greatly alleviated, but not entirely solved, its internal problems; at the same time it has created other, often more complex, dilemmas. Past outbreaks of dissidence have been well-handled by the Kuwaiti authorities. Police and security forces have shown effectiveness and restraint when tacing large demonstrations or hostility toward foreigners in Kuwait. They have not in recent times been tested by any seriously violent outbreaks. Should this occur, there is no way of telling how effective the authorities would be and what the reaction of countries in the region would be in coming to Kuwait's rescue. Recent Iranian-promoted terrorism in Kuwait provides increased cause for concern.

The Kuwaiti government is keenly aware of the potentially destabilizing factor inherent in its large, disenfranchised Palestinian population. Short of granting them blanket citizenship, which Kuwaitis are overwhelmingly unwilling to do, they have attempted with varying success to co-opt them and other aliens with financial rewards. They have offered citizenship on a limited basis. This, so far, has kept the Palestinians from becoming security problem, but their second-class status is a source of frustration to the younger, Kuwaiti-born Palestinians. Their bitterness is exacerbated by the overbearing, high-handed manner with which some Kuwaitis treat other Arabs, the exorbitant rents charged by Kuwaiti landlords, and by inequitable salaries paid to non-Kuwaiti government employees. While the resident alien problem is long-term and without simple solutions, the prospects for its remaining manageable are good unless some major external crisis sweeps Kuwait into a situation in which the traditional constraints – financial reward and fear of extradition – lose effectiveness. As of early 1984 the new militancy of PLO splinter groups and the loosing of radical Islamic forces reacting to American foreign policy in the Middle East, particularly in Lebanon, present new dangers.

There are no large gaps between social classes as in Saudi Arabia, where extremes of wealth have so far caused class distinction. The fine gradation in Kuwait is the fruit of careful policies to raise up Kuwait's poor and unskilled class (through housing, free business sites, obligatory Kuwaiti participation in foreign businesses, etc.) and to give the immigrants reasonable rewards through salaries, while keeping away undesirables and unneeded foreign elements. This necessitated an administration of some skill, which Kuwait acquired early, thanks to the Palestinian immigrants who have filled the middle ranks of an administration headed by Kuwaitis. Social differences in absolute terms between top and bottom may be nearly as great as they are in Saudi Arabia, but the difference lies in the presence of many middle levels between these extremes which form one coherent whole. Because everybody participates (even if unequally), it is a structure which retains its cohesion.

4.2 THE RESPONSE OF THE RULING FAMILY. In a relative sense, the Al Sabah who rule Kuwait have been more willing to "open up" the political system than have the Al Saud of Saudi Arabia or the Al Khalifa of Bahrain. A quarter-century of continuing socioeconomic change in Kuwait makes some sort of accommodation with increased pressures for political participation necessary. Nevertheless, the Al Sabah seem basically unwilling to embark on any serious experiment in power-sharing or to alter radically the existing political foundations of the state. Only a direct threat to their preeminent position would appear to shake Al Sabah complacency. Such a serious threat is not probable for the near future.

4.3 EXTERNAL INFLUENCES. External influences, over which the regime has little or no control, will be a major determinant in the future stability of the country. There are a number of scenarios which could spark major civil disturbances by Kuwait's Palestinian community. These include a precipitous deterioration in the Arab-Israeli situation, (e.g. renewed hostilities), or a major crisis involving Palestinians, such as large-scale expulsions from the West Bank, renewed civil war, an Israeli invasion of Jordan or further incursion in Lebanon. Kuwait's two neighbors to the north also present a continued threat.

The Iraqi threat has been neutralized, at least for the duration of the Iran-Iraq war. The war itself, however, constitutes a threat since in the event of an escalation the first Iranian target is likely to be Kuwait. The emirate is the closest GCC state to Iran, its oil and industrial installations are densely concentrated providing easy targets, and there is little likelihood that the U.S. would or could intervene in Kuwait's behalf or that Saudi Arabia could do so effectively. In light of new threats of escalation of the Iran-Iraq conflict and the uncertain aftermath of American policy failure in Lebanon, which in early 1984 caused Arab moderates to distance themselves from Washington, there are new uncertainties facing Kuwait. The policy of low-profiled neutrality on the regional and international scene and astute use of Kuwaiti wealth may continue to provide security, but the environment has grown more dangerous.

III. ECONOMIC ANALYSIS

1.
SUMMARY CONCLUSIONS

1.1 THE OIL SECTOR. Kuwait was one of the first countries to maximize the returns from its oil wealth. However, Kuwait is not eager to maximize its revenue from oil when the financial return it can realize on its investments falls short of the gain for delaying oil depletion; in other words, Kuwait follows a coherent policy of long-term return maximization. A ceiling of 1.25 mbd is in effect, but Kuwait produced below that level in 1982 and 1983 when its OPEC quota fell below that level. Kuwait has sought to raise sales by asking for and getting an increase in its OPEC quota to 1.05 mbd, at which level it is expected to continue production. Kuwait has established a variety of industries, ranging from prefabricated housing to shipping. It is currently engaged in consolidation of downstream activities for the oil industry through a program of foreign acquisitions.

1.2 THE FINANCIAL SECTOR. Kuwait has a relatively well developed financial sector. Thanks to a carefully executed rescue effort, the sector is recovering from the collapse of the parallel stock market in 1982, the aftereffects of which continue to be felt in all sectors of the economy. Commercial banks have continued to grow despite asset problems. The domestic KD (Kuwaiti Dinar) bond has recently shown signs of reviving. Kuwaiti investment companies continue to be active in the international bond and loan syndication markets, although activities and profits have abated. Foreign assets held by the government (estimated at $72 billion) make Kuwait a major factor in international markets. The income from these assets has declined somewhat, but the decline appears to have been arrested. Foreign aid commitments have been reduced, but the loan component has not diminished significantly.

1.3 NON-OIL SECTORS. Currently the oil sector dominates the economy, accounting for more than 50 percent of nominal GDP. The development of the non-oil sectors has been slow. Neither manufacturing nor agriculture is likely to grow to the point of meaningful diversification. Construction, which has suffered because of low liquidity, is not likely to recover spectacularly, although the need for infrastructural maintenance insures that the construction sector will continue to be of some importance. The Iran-Iraq war has had a major effect on nearly all non-oil sectors – both directly (as re-export trade has stagnated) and indirectly (as investor confidence is eroded). Regional integration through the GCC may improve the prospects for Kuwaiti industry somewhat.

1.4 SOCIAL WELFARE. Kuwait is a working mixture of free enterprise and public welfare. Every Kuwaiti citizen is entitled to free housing, education, and medical care. These benefits are not enjoyed to the same degree by the foreign workers who dominate the workforce. The economic "rationalization" policy favored by the outgoing Finance Minister was to have saved money by making Kuwaitis pay for some of these services. Since his departure, the execution of that policy is doubtful.

1.5 MANPOWER. More than half of Kuwait's population is foreign. The workforce comprises many Arabs, Europeans and Americans as well as Asians who dominate the construction and services sector. Few foreigners living in Kuwait are ever granted Kuwaiti citizenship. The government has grown intolerant of the dependence on foreign labor. It has cracked down on illegal residents, causing labor costs to rise. The foreign workforce, however, shows no sign of shrinking.

1.6 SHORT-TERM OUTLOOK. A moderate recovery is expected after the negative growth of the past two years. According to optimistic forecasts, a GDP increment of up to 10 percent in real terms is possible in the immediate aftermath of the recession, to be followed by a steady growth rate of 4 percent barring major shocks. The current account should continue to show a modest (by Kuwaiti standards) surplus, as oil production stabilizes at a level about the current 1.05 mbd, reaching the ceiling of 1.25 mbd only if international market conditions improve. The liquidity shortage should become less severe, although the channeling of funds abroad may nullify the effects on the domestic economy. The Kuwaiti economy will continue to be heavily dependent on oil. Kuwait's current account balance should show a comfortable surplus, a significant portion of which will be invested abroad. The immediate future of the Kuwaiti economy is heavily dependent on the outcome of the Iran-Iraq war, which threatens Kuwaiti shipping and oil exports, as well as regional stability. A dramatic increase in the intensity of hostilities – or active involvement of Kuwait in the fighting – would necessitate drastic revision of all predictions about the Kuwaiti economy.

2.
MACRO-ECONOMIC ANALYSIS

2.1 THE IMPORTANCE OF OIL AND LABOR. The Kuwaiti economy, once based on fishing, pearling, and trade, now revolves around the oil sector. Oil has provided needed development financing while expatriate workers have provided skilled labor. Since the 1960s, the oil sector has accounted for about two-thirds of Kuwait's GDP. Currently, expatriates make up over half the population of Kuwait.

2.2 DIVERSIFICATION OF THE ECONOMY. Until the early sixties, Kuwait was primarily involved in building its infrastructure; roads, water supplies, power generation, ports, housing, schools, and medical facilities were emphasized. By the mid-sixties, after completing many infrastructure projects, Kuwaiti authorities directed their efforts toward diversifying the industrial base. The trade and service sectors expanded, and many industrial facilities for producing commodities such as chemicals, building materials, foodstuffs, furniture and paper were established.

Following the steady increase of the contribution of the oil sector to total GDP in the fifties, the distribution between oil and non-oil GDP was fairly stable, except for the effect of the quadrupling of oil prices in 1973.

The contribution of the oil sector to GDP has since fluctuated. Much of the fluctuation was due to erratic oil revenues which could not be controlled by, and did not result from, prior planning. Some of the fluctuation, however, must be ascribed to a modest success of the policy of diversification. Representing 79 percent of GDP in 1975, the contribution of the oil sector to GDP fell to 66 percent in 1976, 62 percent in 1977 and 60 percent in 1978. The abrupt increase in oil revenue as a result of higher oil prices altered the situation in 1979, raising the contribution of the oil sector to GDP to 69 percent and 68 percent in 1979 and 1980 respectively. With the decline in oil revenue in the early eighties, the percentage dropped to 61 percent in 1981 and 48.5 percent in

1982. The increase in oil exports in 1983, brought about largely by the acquisition of retail outlets for refined products overseas, caused the share of the oil sector in GDP to grow slightly, to an estimated 49.8 percent.

GDP Growth and Allocation. GDP growth has been erratic, influenced above all by the developments in the oil sector, which still dominates the economy. While nominal GDP has risen steadily – except in 1975 (when the first oil boom ran out of steam) and in 1981 and 1982 (when recession resulted from oil revenue losses) – real GDP has moved more erratically.

Real Expenditure GDP

Year	%Change	Year	%Change	Year	%Change
1973	-3	1976	+13	1979	+11
1974	-7	1977	+2	1980	-10
1975	-2	1978	+6	1981	-2.5

The pattern of change for real expenditure on GDP is interesting. It took Kuwait several years to translate the first oil boom (triggered by higher oil revenues in 1973) into real, meaningful growth. By the time the second oil boom struck (triggered by the increase in oil prices in 1979 and 1980), Kuwait had established a pattern of steady growth. The pattern was destabilized by the shocks of 1979 and 1980; as the government sought to conserve its oil resource, the accelerated growth of the second oil boom turned into negative growth.

Total consumption has grown steadily, if unevenly, in real terms over the past ten years. While both government and private consumption have been growing, private consumption has grown much faster; it almost tripled in real terms in 1981, averaging a 33 percent real growth rate annually.

Given the economy's limited ability to meet consumption needs through production, imports had to be increased. Over a ten year period imports increased nearly fivefold in real terms, registering real growth every year (except for 1978, when infrastructural constraints came into play), and averaging a real growth rate of nearly 50 percent over the same period.

Gross fixed capital formation has also grown impressively in real terms, implying that a significant portion of the wealth generated by oil has been channeled not to consumption but to investment. Gross fixed capital formation nearly quadrupled over the period, averaging a real growth rate of 44 percent annually. This suggests that the absorptive capacity of the economy is fairly impressive, although it should be noted that much of the accumulated wealth was not in fact absorbed but channeled abroad in accordance with a deliberate policy to diversify income sources, as evidenced by massive government foreign assets (estimated at $72 billion) and commercial bank assets (estimated at KD 2.301 billion [$7.865 billion] at the end of 1983).

2.3 THE NON-OIL SECTOR. Within the non-oil sector, the relative shares of many sectors have tended to be quite stable; for example, the shares of agriculture, transportation, finance, and other services remained constant through most of the seventies. Manufacturing, however, almost doubled in its relative share of GDP during that period. The bulk of the share of industrial production, has consisted of hydrocarbon based industries, and the prices of hydrocarbon products have increased much faster than the general price index. If one defines the manufacturing sector to exclude petrochemicals (as we shall do in this analysis), the picture is very different.

In 1981, the manufacturing sector declined (it registered a growth rate of -15.25 percent), the parallel stock market (Manakh) crash having shattered private sector confidence and reduced liquidity. While the sector rallied somewhat in 1983 (growing by 7.4 percent after registering practically no change in 1982), it still accounted for no more than 6.4 percent of GDP in 1983. Agriculture has likewise proved sluggish; it continues to account for less than 1 percent of GDP, reflecting the unfavorable prospects for agricultural development. Trade, a traditional occupation in Kuwait as in all Gulf states, maintained its steady but unspectacular growth in the early eighties, suggesting that its share of GDP will remain under ten percent. Construction, which boomed through the mid-seventies and then experienced reduced growth in the late seventies, maintained a share in the range of 5 percent of GDP.

Among the sectors registering unusual growth in the early eighties, financial insitutions were the most impressive; they grew by 28 percent in 1981, 25 percent in 1982, and 11.1 in 1983. They accounted for 4.8 percent of GDP in 1983, their continued robust growth in the shadow of the Manakh crash being an indication of continued government and Central Bank support. Transport, storage and communications grew at 17 percent in 1981, 25 percent in 1982, and 11.2 percent in 1983, a remarkable growth in view of the unenthusiastic attitude toward the development of transportation facilities fostered by the Iran-Iraq war.

The relative share and overall growth rates of all sectors are likely to be heavily dependent on the course of the Iraq-Iran war. Any disruption of Gulf shipping would have a major effect on the economy, reducing (or halting) oil exports and putting enormous pressure on the non-oil sectors. Even a modest increase in the level of tension is likely to cause serious difficulties in all sectors, as investor confidence is severely tested and the shipping of oil exports and various imports is affected.

Gross Domestic Product at Current Prices
1978-83
(KD million)

	1979	1980	1981	1982	1983
Oil Sector	4,420.4	5,062.3	4,125.1	2,766.7	3,094.0
Non-Oil Sector	2,323.0	2,389.9	2,647.1	2,960.8	3,124.7
Agriculture & Fisheries	16.7	17.3	28.0	31.0	34.0
Manufacturing	574.3	439.9	372.8	373.4	401.0
Electricity, Gas, & Water	26.6	25.0	26.8	30.1	34.1
Construction	210.0	220.0	263.0	283.0	289.0
Wholesale & Retail Trade	426.0	468.0	485.0	521.0	508.0
Transport, Storage, & Communications	106.4	124.3	145.5	171.8	191.0
Financial Institutions	135.3	169.0	216.3	270.0	300.0
Insurance	13.3	14.5	16.0	18.0	19.0
Other	814.4	910.8	1,093.7	1,262.5	1,348.6
GDP	6,743.4	7,451.2	6,772.2	5,727.5	6,218.7

Source: Ministry of Planning, Central Statistical Office

2.4 MONETARY SURVEY (1974-1978). The sharp increase in the price of oil in 1973-74 led to a substantial increase in government revenue, which resulted in huge surpluses. Although the real price of crude (adjusted for inflation) thereafter declined in real terms until 1979, the government's main concern was to match its expenditure to its revenue. The massive increase in government revenue resulted in what the government later regarded as an unhealthy growth of the public sector. Furthermore, the absorptive capacity of the economy was strained to the limit; the infrastructural constraint on imports was dramatized by port congestion in 1977. During that period, the money supply (defined as demand deposits plus currency in circulation) more than tripled in size (from KD 195.6 million [$698.3 million] in 1974 to KD 636.4 million [2.341 billion] in 1978). This was equivalent to an annual growth rate of approximately 35 percent. It did not, however, result in excessive inflation; over the same period, the average inflation rate (defined as the percentage change in the consumer price index) stood at approximately 9 percent annually. This can be explained by the fact that Kuwait's development, unlike that of most developing countries, has not been constrained by lowering savings levels. Its oil revenues and its relatively low consumption capacities created a savings/GDP ratio in excess of 50 percent in the 1970s. (This ratio peaked at 74 percent in 1973-74.) Both Kuwait's low investment potential and the desire to diversify income sources by acquiring an extensive portfolio of foreign assets have held back its ratio of I/GDP. Consequently, a significant portion of Kuwaiti revenues are invested abroad. In 1978 the foreign assets of the commercial banking system were more than three quarters of commercial banking credit in the private sector.

2.5 RECENT DEVELOPMENTS (1978-1982). The dramatic increase in oil revenues in 1979 increased pressure on aggregate demand. The money supply (defined as money plus quasi-money) increased by 17 percent, government deposits which had been declining increased by a whopping 52 percent, while claims on the private sector grew by 36 percent, signaling the beginning of an unprecedented boom. The accelerated increase in all monetary aggregates was bound to intensify inflationary pressure after the usual lag; while inflation was no more than 5 percent in 1979, it jumped to 14.5 percent in 1980. The foreign assets held by commercial banks rose 41.7 percent.

Monetary growth accelerated further in 1980, as the money supply increased 21 percent, while government deposits at commercial banks continued their rapid increase at 43 percent. The boom continued as commercial banks increased their claims on the private sector by 29 percent, and foreign assets by 22 percent.

By 1981, there was perceptible concern in government circles about the direction of the economy. Investors were gripped by an endless boom mentality; speculation, especially in stocks on the parallel market, became rife. The money supply was growing at 36 percent, and claims on the private sector at 24 percent. Inflation was kept under control (7.3 percent in 1981) through heavy consumer goods subsidization and booming imports; its 1982 level likewise was a mere 7.8 percent.

Monetary growth was, however, deliberately slowed down by the monetary authorities. The money supply grew only 8 percent in 1982, and while government deposits were allowed to grow 35 percent, they had fallen 6 percent in the previous year. The boom was coming to an end, but speculators refused to believe it. Claims on the private sector continued to expand, growing by 24 percent in 1982. More alarmingly, speculation and inadequate liquidity created a market for postdated checks as a means of obtaining supplementary credit. This was bound to result in an explosion, which it did, in the form of the Manakh crash in the late summer and fall of 1982.

2.6 PROJECTIONS. The economy has yet to recover from the impact of the crash. The situation is compounded by the following complications:

- Oil revenues declined in the early eighties, rallying only recently. As these constitute the major source of government revenue, and the latter is the propelling force in the economy, this has deepened the recession.
- The stock market has been stagnant, despite vigorous efforts by the government and the banking sector (see below) to revive it. Most stock prices are well below their peak 1982 levels – an indication of the continuing recession and prevailing gloom in business circles.
- Since the Manakh crash and even before it, the government, and the Finance Ministry in particular, favored austerity measures and economic "rationalization." While such an attitude has been praised by international experts, it has done little to boost the confidence of a private sector accustomed to thriving on government largesse.
- The Iraq-Iran war since 1979 has posed physical danger to Kuwait (in the form of threats of Iranian retaliation for Kuwaiti backing of Iraq, as well as the oil slick which menaced marine life in the Gulf).

This has hindered Gulf trade, and created an atmosphere of instability.

- Kuwait's support for Iraq involves heavy financial contributions which have proved a heavy drain on Kuwaiti finances and damaged the soundness of Kuwait's international portfolio. The contributions have largely been suspended, although non-cash assistance (debt settlements in Iraq's behalf) is believed by some to have taken place recently.
- The overall instability in the region has affected Kuwait; domestic terrorism, fostered partly by the general sense of malaise prevailing in the Arab world since the Israeli invasion of Lebanon in 1982 and partly by Iranian propaganda, has further eroded confidence.
- The Kuwaiti dinar is under considerable pressure. The exchange rate in mid-1984 was KD 0.297 to a dollar (compared with KD 0.291 to a dollar at the end of 1983). This is a direct result of the large capital transfers abroad by nervous investors. While the government has responded by imposing limitations on large capital transfers, many fear the exchange rate may deteriorate further, passing the KD 0.300 mark in the near future.
- The dimunition of the domestic market and the uncertain condition of the regional market are likely to lead to more bankruptcies; indeed, a fair number of businesses in Kuwait (as in other Gulf states) are believed to be bankrupt in all but name. The cost to the government of bailing out these insitutions or placing them under the guardianship of the Industrial Bank of Kuwait would be a major burden.

At the same time, there are some positive signs:

- Efforts at economic integration in the Gulf region are making significant headway. A customs union is already in effect, which augurs well for the development of Kuwait's industrial sector.
- The government is committed to maintaining existing infrastructure and proceeding with some development projects in spite of the austere mood. This, together with measures that favor Kuwaiti contractors, sustains the construction sector.
- The tentative settlement of postdated checks early this year has restored a measure of confidence in the financial sector. This sector has recovered to some extent from the shock of the resignation of the Finance Minister, Abd al-Latif al-Hamad,late last

year. The government has already spent an estimated KD 750 million ($2.567 billion) on the stock market to prop up demand, and the commercial banking sector has become involved in efforts to firm stock prices through the recent formation of a financial institution with a capital of KD 600 million ($2.051 billion) (to be owned by commercial banks) to buy stocks on the market. Liquidity available to investors has also increased somewhat as a result of huge sums (an estimated KD 3 billion) ($10.3 billion) being disbursed by the government as compensation to small investors hurt by the Manakh crash.

- The newly proposed Kuwaiti budget (for 1984-85) is expected to have a largely expansionary impact. The increase in the budget allocation for development is considered encouraging, particularly for the construction sector.
- The money supply is now growing at a reasonable rate (4 percent in 1983) to reach KD 4.368 billion ($14.930 billion) at year's end, a slight decline in real terms. Government deposits declined slightly in 1983, reducing available liquidity but averting renewed inflationary pressure. Inflation in 1983 was 4.7 percent. Claims on the private sector have continued to grow (11 percent in 1983), as have the foreign assets of commercial banks, which increased 2.2 percent to the level of KD 2.301 billion ($7.866 billion) at the end of 1983.

Recently released figures indicate that 1983 was a disastrous year. The growth rate of the non-oil sector fell to 5.5 percent, the construction sector showed nearly no growth, and the trade sector fell in terms of its contribution to GDP by 3 percent. Imports fell (for the first time in recent years) by 9 percent. While such developments may signal a low-growth attitude discouraging domestic investment, they can also be taken as a sign of stabilization, and possible controlled economic growth in the future.

3.
DEVELOPMEMT PLANNING

3.1 THE PLANNING PROCESS Planning for development has been largely ignored in the past. Two five-year plans were drawn up but not pursued. A third five-year plan, 1976-81, projected expenditures of KD 1 billion ($3.57 billion) in both the oil sector and the private sector and KD 2.3 billion ($8.2 billion) for other ministries and autonomous agencies. At the conclusion of the planning period, performance was well below target.

Although Kuwait needs coherent policies and planning, the urgency for these is lessened by Kuwait's immense capital assets and by the free enterprise spirit overwhelmingly present in the economy. In addition, Kuwait can afford to emphasize public welfare in its development. Every Kuwaiti citizen is entitled to free housing, education, and medical care.

Part of Kuwait's problem with long-range planning lies in the difficulty of predicting revenue and expenses. Oil revenues have fluctuated wildly in the past two years. As oil prices increased dramatically in late 1979 as a result of the Iranian revolution, the government was compelled to increase output for purely political reasons. Expenses are largely uncontrollable. Foreign suppliers, who play a crucial role in Kuwait's development, have sometimes increased prices unexpectedly; for example, the cost of three electric schemes increased 23.5 percent in January 1981, $1.02 billion more than previously estimated. This necessitated an additional budget allocation.

The government does not view the growth of the public sector with favor. This has not prevented the government from imposing monetary controls when the need arose, from enlarging the role of the Central Bank, or from nationalizing the Kuwait Oil Tanker Company (KOTC) in 1979 to better organize the oil sector.

3.2 PLANNING GOALS At present, Kuwait has no formal economic development plan. Planning strategies do exist in a number of areas, in particular, the oil industry, industrial development, infrastructural development, electricity and water supply, and public services. The intentions of planners, as revealed by these strategies, can be summarized as follows:

- Developing the downstream activities of the oil industry, through expansion of refining facilities, increased oil transportation capacity, and the acquisition of retail outlets overseas.
- Diversifying state income through the development of new industries, and, particularly, promoting the financial sector in order to generate revenue from other sources than hydrocarbons.
- Improving the nation's infrastructure (transport and communications), and maintaining all existing infrastructure.
- Increasing the supply of electricity and desalinated water to meet increasing demand.
- Improving public services and providing these to the Kuwaiti public at minimal cost.
- Providing adequate public housing for all needy Kuwaitis.
- Promoting the participation of private investment in local production.

3.3 PERFORMANCE. Due to a number of complications (fluctuating oil revenues, lack of coordination and competition among planners, limited opportunities for domestic industrial development, the difficulty of forecasting revenue and expenditure) Kuwait's record in achieving its objectives is mixed. In particular:

- Kuwait has proven remarkably successful in penetrating foreign, particularly European, markets for oil products. This has contributed to the development of the oil industry's downstream activities. It remains to be seen whether this record can be maintained in the face of increasing hostility on the part of buyers, and the prospect of intense competition.
- It has proved difficult for Kuwait to develop a meaningful industrial base because of labor shortages, the difficulty of technological transfer, inadequate resources, and the small domestic market. Diversification through industrialization, therefore, seems increasingly unfeasible in the near future.
- A formidable financial sector has been developed. While domestic financial institutions were badly

shaken by the financial crash of 1982, which demonstrated their vulnerability and strong dependence on government support, government revenue from foreign reserves (which are believed to total $72 billion) has been high enough (estimated at KD 1.300 billion [$4.443 billion] in 1982-83) to constitute a major source of revenue, indicating some success in diversifying state income sources.

- Considerable infrastructural development has been achieved. The government has been meticulous about insuring that maintenance of existing infrastructure is adequately covered in the state budget, the mood of fiscal conservatism notwithstanding.
- The supply of electricity has been boosted from 5.7 billion KWH in 1976 to 10.3 billion KWH in 1981, while the supply of water has been more than doubled from 55.004 MCM in 1975 to 115.92 MCM in 1981. Artificially low prices have caused consumption to grow even faster; the budget of the Ministry of Electricity and Water is the largest and fastest-growing of Kuwaiti ministerial budgets. While the pragmatically-minded new Finance Minister, Shaikh Ali, decided to postpone price increases for water and electricity, the Electricity and Water Ministry has started a major advertising campaign to encourage conservation of water and power by the public.
- An impressive range of public services (including free or nearly free public housing) continues to be supplied by government agencies to all Kuwaiti citizens. Non-citizens are not eligible for the same free benefits, which has contributed to expatriate discontent.
- The private sector has been slow to invest in industrial development, which continues to be dominated by the public sector.
- The Manakh crash in 1982 eroded private sector confidence. While the liquidity of the private sector may have improved, it is not at all certain that much of it will find its way to domestic investments.

3.4 INFRASTRUCTURAL DEVELOPMENT. Public investment programs, especially in infrastructure formation, started in Kuwait much earlier than in the other Gulf countries. The first plan for the development of Kuwait City was issued in the early fifties; by the mid-sixties Kuwait had already laid down a relatively advanced infrastructure.

Kuwait was generally ahead of other Gulf oil producers in recognizing the need for economic diversification.

The early attempts at industrialization began with the formation of the National Industries Company in 1969, which was a mixed-sector (private and public) company and has been primarily engaged in the production of building materials.

The development of infrastructure and the expansion of industrial output has acted as a catalyst for the development of the trade and service sector. This sector is not directly influenced by public policy; rather, it is essentially driven by the private sector and is dominated by an active re-export market (very heavily dependent on the course of the Iraq-Iran war, by which it has already been adversely affected) and expanding financial and banking services activities.

3.5 STATE BUDGET (PROJECTED REVENUE AND EXPENDITURE).

Public policy, as reflected in the state budget, is perceived as having three objectives:

- The provision of essential public services
- Transferring wealth to poorer Kuwaitis
- Boosting level of aggregate spending when necessary

The latter objective has increased in significance since the Manakh crash, which eroded confidence in the Kuwaiti economy, triggered a wave of bankruptcies, and resulted in a severe liquidity shortage. Heavy government spending to boost aggregate demand has arisen since the oil glut began and the Iran-Iraq war narrowed the range of business activity and triggered a slowdown.

As a result, budget deficits have been the norm since 1981-82. It should be noted that the "deficit" stems from an accounting practice: revenue from foreign investments (accumulated reserves) is automatically rolled over to the General Reserve Fund, an off-budget item. That revenue was officially reported to be KD 1.364 billion ($4.724 billion) in 1981-82 and is expected (conservatively) to be KD 1.300 billion ($4.502 billion) in 1982-83, more than ample to cover the deficits reported for those fiscal years.

For 1982-83, the deficit is estimated at KD 312 million ($1.0807 billion) (lower than earlier projections of KD 400 million [$1.385 billion] or more). The deficit is projected to increase to KD 851 million ($2.909 billion) for 1983-84, or nearly 28 percent of revenues. Note that the the 1982-83 figure includes KD 150 million ($519.6 million) (decided in January 1983) for land acquisitions.

Kuwaiti Budget
1982/83 – 1984/85
(KD million)

Expenditure:	1984/85	%Change	1983/84	%Change	1982/83
General:	3,654.0	8.2	3,376.0	6.6	3,168.0
Wages and Salaries	725.0	0.7	719.9	14.9	3,168.0
Other Running Expenses	515.0	-0.4	517.2	29.3	400.0
Transport and Equipment	32.0	-16.7	38.4	-23.2	50.0
Development Schemes	858.0	29.5	662.4	9.9	603.0
Land Expropriations	150.0	--	150.0	--	150.0
Unclassified and Transfers	1,374.0	6.6	1,288.0	-3.5	1,335.0
Reserve Fund for Future Generations	322.7	--	303.7	--	320.6
Total	**4,067.7**	**8.0**	**3,710.0**	**5.4**	**3,518.6**
Revenue:	1984/85	%Change	1983/84	%Change	1982/83
Oil	2,912.0	4.5	2,787.6	-6.0	2,967.0
Other	314.5	26.1	249.4	4.4	239.0
Total	**3,227.0**	**6.3**	**3,037.0**	**-5.3**	**3,206.0**
Deficit	779.7		673.0		312.6

Source: Kuwaiti News Agency (KUNA)

The major elements of public policy revealed in the 1983-84 budget are:

- In response to projected declining revenues from oil sales (a 5.6 percent decline from the previous fiscal year) the fiscal austerity implied in the "rationalization" policy of outgoing Finance Minister al-Hamad continues to be implemented after his resignation; expenditure is projected to grow only 8.4 percent.
- The allocation for the Reserve Fund for the Future has been decreased slightly. This reflects the

impossibility of maintaining government savings at their previously high level.

- Almost all ministries have received an increased allocation, the Ministry of Electricity and Water being the beneficiary of the largest increase in absolute amount (a 34.6 percent increase). The latter Ministry, together with those of Defense, Public Works, Public Health and Education, remain the major recipients of government funds and have received major increases in allocation.
- Considerable reorganization has occurred: electric power stations and water desalination stations have been merged in the Ministry of Water and Electricity; five new agencies were created with attached budgets (Fire Department, Public Savings, Vocational Training, Amiri Palace Administration, and an Agency for Financial Settlement of Postdated Checks); a new Zakat (Religious Charity) House was created with an independent budget.
- The Lending and Saving Agency, Kuwait Airlines and the Kuwait Institute for Scientific Research were given greater latitude in expenditure policy.
- The Kuwait Fund for Arab Economic Development (KFAED), Kuwait's international aid agency, received a KD 30 million ($102.5 million) increase in capital (same amount as in last budget), an indication of continued state support.

3.6 FISCAL OPERATIONS (ACTUAL REVENUE AND EXPENDITURE). An examination of fiscal operations indicates a fluctuating level of revenue from oil, reflecting changing conditions in oil markets and deliberate decisions to cut or boost production. In the first quarter of 1983-84 (which coincided with the summer quarter of 1983), oil revenue registered a substantial increase to KD 661.8 million ($2.266 billion) from KD 497.3 million ($1.703 billion) in the previous quarter; oil revenues increased markedly in September 1983 (to KD 263.1 million [$905.75 million] for the month) as a result of improving conditions in the international oil market.

Total expenditure has increased steadily since 1975-76. In the first quarter of 1983-84 it recorded a decline of 14.6 percent from the previous quarter, reflecting seasonal reductions in development expenditure (a 36.3 percent decline) and expropriation outlays (a 43.2 percent decline); this was partially offset by a substantial increase in expenditure for foreign transfers, which reached KD 95.7 million ($327.6 million) (compared to KD 24.4 million ($83.53 million) in the previous quarter) because of the timing of Arab aid commitments.

3.7 PROPOSED BUDGET. A budget for 1984-85 (which has yet to be approved by Parliament) was approved by the cabinet on April 15. It calls for a deficit of KD 779.7 million ($2.661 billion) (16 percent higher than the deficit initially approved for 1983-84). Some, particularly in the press, have criticized this as fiscally irresponsible, tantamount to liquidating reserves in order to meet current needs. On the other hand, many have taken heart from the expansionary implications of the widening deficit. Particularly heartening is the observation that development expenditure is being boosted, the amount allocated to development schemes being 29.5 percent higher than last year.

Overall revenue is projected to rise by 6.3 percent. Oil revenue is projected to increase by 4.5 percent as a result of Kuwait's modest success in increasing exports. Non-oil revenues, while they are projected to increase by 26.1 percent, remain quite small, accounting for less than 10 percent of all revenue. Increased charges on water and electricity would have substantially altered the situation but were postponed for political reasons.

Overall expenditure is to rise by 8.0 percent in the projected 1984-85 budget. The only allocations to be cut are "other running expenses" (current expenses other than wages and salaries) which will fall slightly, and spending on transport and equipment, to be cut 16.7 percent. Much of the increase in general expenditure will be allocated to defense, a reflection of the growing tension in the region. A measure of fiscal conservatism is illustrated by the low growth of wages and salaries (0.7 percent, compared with 14.3 percent last year), a result of deliberate attrition in jobs held by non-Kuwaitis.

The magnitude of the deficit is misleading; many of the projected allocations (e.g to the Reserve Fund and KFAED capital) represent accounting (non-cash) transfers. Furthermore, income from Kuwait's foreign investment (projected to continue at about the same level of 1982-83, namely KD 1.300 billion [$4.443 billion]) is excluded from the budget; if included, it would turn the deficit into a not inconsiderable surplus.

4. PETROLEUM SECTOR

4.1 GENERAL CONDITION OF THE INDUSTRY. Although the oil sector experienced negative growth in 1982, registering a growth rate of -32.5 percent, Kuwait's economy still revolves around the oil sector. Petroleum and gas production account for more than 48.5 percent of GDP, while sales of crude oil and gas account for 88 percent of government revenues, and 82 percent of export earnings.

Kuwaiti oil wells have an installed capacity estimated at 2.9 mbd, with a maximum sustainable capacity of 2.5 mbd. In 1972 an upper ceiling of 2 mbd was imposed to prevent too rapid a depletion of Kuwait's most valuable resource. The ceiling was revised to 1.5 mbd in April 1980, and subsequently to 1.25 mbd. At current production levels (1.08 mbd in January 1984, slightly in excess of its OPEC quota of 1.05 mbd), proven reserves (estimated at 69 billion barrels, making Kuwait the third largest in the world in oil reserves) are expected to last for as long as 180 years. Oil income for 1984 is projected at $10.4 billion, slightly higher than the 1983 level of $10.3 billion. Kuwaiti oil is heavier and has a higher sulphur content than Saudi oil, but Kuwaiti oil is produced under very favorable conditions, as evidenced by its low production cost, $0.15 per barrel. In 1983, domestic consumption of oil was estimated at 0.169 mbd.

Natural gas is produced jointly with oil. The gas is partly reinjected into the wells to maintain reservoir pressure and partly used for domestic industry; 40 percent is flared. Proven reserves of natural gas are 90.624 million cu m. Production dropped sharply because of falling oil production; in 1982 it amounted to 4.588 billion cu m (compared to a peak of 12.027 billion cu m in 1979). Kuwait has imported gas in recent years to make up the shortfall in feedstock supplies.

Natural gas production is expected to be expanded as a result of the southern gas project awarded to France's Technip in 1983. The project entails the gathering and compression of associated gas produced from the offshore Khafji oilfield in the Neutral Zone (which is jointly owned with Saudi Arabia). An onshore gas treatment plant and pipeline will be built to transport the gas to the Mina al-Ahmadi LPG plant.

4.2 OIL REFINING AND SHIPPING. Kuwait has succeeded in increasing the percentage of crude that is refined before final sales. Even in years when crude sales have plummeted, exports of refined product have climbed, amounting to a value of KD 945 million ($3,230.1 million) in 1983 (32 percent of total oil exports).

There are three refineries (at Mina al-Ahmadi, Mina Abdullah and Shuaiba). The refinery at Mina al-Ahmadi is being modernized by the Japan Gasoline Corporation, while the Mina Abdullah refinery is being expanded by Kuwait Santa Fe Braun. While refining exports were estimated at 0.4 mbd in April and May of 1983 (compared to 0.45 mbd in February), Kuwait's oil refining capacity is currently estimated at 0.6 mbd of which 0.08-0.1 mbd is destined for local consumption. Refining capacity is projected to increase to nearly 0.7 mbd by 1986, bringing Kuwait closer to the goal of refining all domestically produced oil.

Kuwait is also seeking to build a large tanker fleet, with the aim (by the mid-eighties according to planners) of having Kuwaiti tankers carry 45 percent of its crude oil exports, 60 percent of its refined products, and 50 percent of its LPG exports. In the summer of 1979, the Kuwait Oil Tanker Company (KOTC) was nationalized. Its capital was increased from KD 25.9 million ($94.8 million) to KD 200 million (732.3 million), with the intention of increasing its fleet (which comprised 14 crude oil carriers and 4 LPG carriers in 1980) by twelve vessels almost immediately. In line with the expansion of refined crude sales, the emphasis has been placed on product tankers. Shipping capacity was 2.5 million dwt at the end of 1981.

4.3 OIL PRODUCTION AND PRICING POLICIES. Since Kuwait began producing oil in the 1940s, oil output has consistently increased. It peaked at 3.3 mbd in 1972, at which time the output ceiling was set. As the following chart indicates, Kuwait's post-1972 output declined from previous levels, even though oil prices quadrupled in 1973 and continued to increase thereafter (except in 1977).

The year 1979 saw a massive increase in oil prices, and enormous speculative demand for oil on the part of consumers. Kuwait's output increased as a result but a conservationist mood prevailed, prompting a drop in oil production in 1980 and 1981 that was entirely in accordance with the objectives of Kuwaiti planners.

The situation in 1982 became more complicated. As financial pressure on Kuwait intensified (Kuwait was then extending considerable financial assistance to Iraq), oil demand slackened and sales plummeted in the face of sharp discounting by other OPEC producers; Kuwait found the average 1982 level of production (0.82 mbd) somewhat lower than desired. Kuwait asked for and was given an increase in its OPEC quota to 1.05 mbd. Although it took some time for production to rise, it stood at a level slightly higher than the quota at the end of 1983.

Kuwait is not a big enough producer to influence the pricing of oil. It has been fairly radical in OPEC meetings, asking for high prices. It has, however, had the advantage of not needing exceptionally high oil revenues, having accumulated international reserves yielding high revenue. This, coupled with Kuwait's obvious interest in insuring the long-term strength of the oil market (given its considerable oil reserves), has caused it to refrain from "cheating" (seriously exceeding its quota or destabilizing prices by discounting).

Crude Oil Production: Update
(thousand bbl)

1975	760,700
1976	785,000
1977	718,100
1978	776,900
1979	911,000
1980	607,200
1981	411,200
1982	72,600
1983	224,100
May	31,800
June	31,200
July	33,600
Aug	36,600
Sept	37,500
Oct	40,500
Nov	38,000
Dec	38,000
1984	
Jan	35,030
Feb	35,815
Mar	39,990
Apr	36,000
May	34,100

Source: Petroleum Economist August 1984

4.4 ORGANIZATION OF THE OIL INDUSTRY. The Kuwaiti government has thoroughly reorganized the oil sector to ensure that there is no wasteful duplication of effort by the various government and semi-private companies responsible for the oil sector. The four Kuwaiti oil companies have been regrouped under the Kuwait Petroleum Corporation (KPC), which was set up in 1980 with an initial capital of KD 1 billion ($3.7 billion), later raised to KD 2.5 billion ($9.2 billion). It is chaired by the Oil Minister, and reports directly to the Higher Petroleum Council.

The four Kuwait oil companies (now under the umbrella of KPC), are:

- The Kuwait Oil Company (KOC), which was formerly owned by British Petroleum and Gulf Oil. It was fully nationalized in 1974-75; BP and Gulf Oil were paid compensation and given privileged access to a large proportion of Kuwaiti oil. As of 1980, the KOC was responsible for all oil and gas production (except in the Neutral Zone, where oil production is operated by a Japanese company). It operates the $1 billion LNG export plant, which produced 4.588 billion cu m of LPG in 1982).
- The Kuwait National Petroleum Company (KNPC), which was set up by the government in 1960, but did not become fully government owned until 1975. It took over from KOC exclusive responsibility for internal distribution of oil products, and, as of 1980, local and international marketing. It also operates a refinery at Shuaiba with a 0.2 mbd capacity, and the Mina Abdullah refinery, which has a 0.125 mbd capacity.
- The Petrochemical Industry Company (PIC), which is wholly government owned. It now manages petrochemical production and various downstream activities. It has a fertilizer division, which operates a petrochemical complex at Shuaiba comprising three ammonia plants (annual capacity: 660,000 metric tons), three urea plants (annual capacity: 792 metric tons), one ammonium sulphate plant (annual capacity: 165,000 metric tons) and one sulphuric acid plant (annual capacity: 132,000 metric tons). Its salt and chlorine division produces 18,600 tons of salt and 9,800 tons of chlorine annually, as well as caustic soda, hydrochloric acid, sodium hypochlorite, compressed hydrogen and distilled water (90 million MCM).
- The Kuwait Oil Tanker Company (KOTC), which was founded in 1957 by private entrepreneurs. The state

took a 49 percent stake in it in 1976, and nationalized it wholly in 1979. Its capital was raised from KD 25.9 million ($94.8 million) to KD 200 million ($732.3 million). As of 1980, it has been responsible for the transportation of crude oil and LPG; twelve new vessels were ordered.

KPC's 1983-84 budget, the second largest after the main government's, projects a net profit of KD 45 million ($153.8 million) (compared to KD 56 million [191.4 million] in 1982-83). Revenues are projected at KD 3.268 billion ($11.170 billion), and expenditures at KD 3.223 billion ($11.016 billion).

4.5 DEVELOPMENT OF OIL SECTOR. The government objectives for the oil sector can be summarized as follows:

- Conservation of the country's hydrocarbon reserves through continued exploration and slow depletion; toward this end the official oil production ceiling was last set at 1.25 mbd.
- Expansion of the productive capacity of all KPC subsidiaries; this entails increasing refining capacity and product-line diversification.
- Using flexible market techniques and tapping new markets.
- Increasing the foreign holdings (overseas investments) of the petroleum sector to bring about a better geographical distribution and diversified downstream activities.

In pursuance of the government objectives, the KPC has undertaken an ambitious program of expansion and, either directly or through its subsidiaries, the acquisition of stakes in foreign companies. Expansion has taken the following form:

- The Kuwait Foreign Petroleum Exploration Company (KUFPEC) was set up with an initial capital of KD 100 million ($341.8 million) to carry out oil exploration and production abroad
- The Kuwait International Petroleum Investment Corporation (KIPIC) was set up with a capital of KD 100 million ($341.8 million) to undertake all overseas investment other than exploration.

Foreign acquisitions have been proceeding at a phenomenal scale, to the point where Kuwait is becoming a force to be reckoned with in the international oil product market. These foreign acquisitions include:

Initial acquisitions:

- 25 percent participation in the International Energy Development Corporation;
- 20 percent of Metallgesellschaft;
- 50 percent of Pacific Resources Incorporated (based in Honolulu) activities in the Pacific Basin;
- Full control of the U.S.-based Santa Fe International. Purchased at $2.5 billion in 1981, its subsidiaries include Santa Fe Drilling Company, Santa Fe Minerals, C.F. Braun (the engineering contractor) and a 16.6 percent stake in the 0.1 mbd British Thistle Field in the North Sea;
- 25 percent of West Germany's Hoechst, acquired in 1982;
- Gulf's Scandinavian and Benelux downstream operations (750 gas stations in Benelux and 800 gas stations in Scandinavia), as well as two Gulf oil refineries and other joint venture arrangements, exploration rights in several LDC's, participation in Heavy Oil Conversion Company of Bahrain, a stake in a joint venture refinery in Malaysia.

Recent downstream investments:

- Pace Petroleum, a UK distributor with 400 gas stations in Britain, which was purchased in late 1983 through Hays Group Ltd. (wholly owned by Kuwait). Hays had formerly acquired Sadler and Company, which supplies 250 stations;
- Gulf downstream operations in Italy (including a 75 percent stake in the closed Sarni refinery, which still has 1,500 outlets and 3.5 percent of the Italian gasoline market);
- A letter of intent signed by PIC with Hoechst to set up an international marketing network for ammonia and chemical fertilizers;
- A 49-percent PIC interest in the Tunisian Gabes Fertilizer Company, which produces mono-ammonium phosphate and liquid ammonia.

4.6 EVALUATION OF DEVELOPMENT STRATEGY. The government's strategy for the devlopment of the oil sector essentially involves Kuwait becoming a major factor in oil product markets by consolidating downstream operations through:

- The expansion of refinery facilities. Kuwait has gone on record as wanting to insure that at least 60 percent of its crude products are refined before sale. It appears that this objective has been achieved.
- Undertaking exploration worldwide and acquiring a stake in other oil production centers. In this the Kuwaitis are encountering considerable resistence, particularly in the United States, where Santa Fe, wholly owned by Kuwait, is being denied drilling rights. In Third World countries which lack capital to develop their oil resources cooperation has been more forthcoming.
- Acquiring control over distribution, thus protecting itself against reversion to a buyers' market. Kuwait has proved spectacularly successful in acquiring retail outlets, particularly in Europe, where it has not been averse to acquiring (directly or indirectly) highly unprofitable oil enterprises merely to insure outlets for Kuwaiti refined crude.

Kuwait is in a position to establish itself in the oil market. Considering how poor the profitability of most European refineries has been, vertical integration seems inevitable in European product markets. The operation of such refineries is much easier when refinery losses are offset by the major revenue from crude sales which accrues to Kuwait.

At the same time, Kuwait is taking a major risk. It is likely to encounter intense competition, not to say outright hostility, in many product markets. Furthermore, Kuwait's success in establishing itself in European product markets could entice other OPEC states (particularly Saudi Arabia) to emulate Kuwait, starting a free for all which could be extremely injurious to Kuwait's financial health.

5.
INDUSTRIAL SECTOR

5.1 GROWTH OF THE INDUSTRIAL SECTOR. Because of the limited potential for agricultural development in Kuwait, the authorities have relied on the industrial sector for diversifying the production base of the economy. The value-added of the manufacturing sector grew at an average rate of 16.28 percent per annum over the 1974-80 period. By 1980, the manufacturing sector (including oil refining) contributed KD 136.5 ($472.8) to GDP at constant 1982 prices, thereby amounting to 8.5 percent of real GDP. In 1981, manufacturing output actually declined (15.25 percent) in nominal terms, being the only sector other than oil to register nominal decline in that year. In 1982, the manufacturing sector registered a negligible growth rate; it underwent a partial recovery in 1983, growing by 7.4 percent. Even so, its total contribution (KD 424.2 million [$472.8 million]) to GDP at in 1983 was a mere 6.4 percent.

5.2 OWNERSHIP AND OUTPUT. The industrial sector in Kuwait is composed of three types of ownership – a government-owned sector, a private sector, and a mixed ownership sector. The petroleum industries – refining, gas liquefication, and petrochemical production – make up the government-owned sector. The mixed sector consists of such industries as building materials, foodstuffs, and paper products; it accounts for about 20 percent (3.5 percent of GDP) of total industrial production.

Private sector establishments account for the bulk of total manufacturing units, exceeding three thousand units, but they generate only 15-20 percent of industrial value added. The majority of these establishments are very small units engaged in basic manufacturing such as textiles, leather goods, clothing (these three constitute 60 percent of private subsector activity), wood products (about 20 percent), food processing, and various handicrafts.

Kuwait's industrial development has relied, and will continue to rely, on hydrocarbon-based industries. Two major reasons for this are the country's natural advantage in energy and petrochemical feedstock, and the fact that these industries are highly capital intensive and thus better to Kuwait's capital abundance and labor shortage.

5.3 STRENGTHS AND WEAKNESSES. The government initially supported the development of nearly any type of industry. Law No. 6 of 1965 offered industrial enterprises a number of privileges and incentives: industrial plots at nominal rent, material support in research and development, infrastructural support (including water, electric power, gas and fuel) at nominal charge, custom-free machinery and supplies, custom protection in certain cases, and short-term loans from the Industrial Bank of Kuwait.

Nonetheless, the relatively poor record of the industrial sector attests to problems which government support could not alleviate:

- The domestic market is small, and a long-standing policy of low tariffs has caused the public to develop a taste for imported products. There is little prospect of sufficient domestic demand to make cost-effective production a serious possibility.
- Raw material imports are often inadequate, largely as a result of poor prior planning.
- A fair amount of imported machinery is unsuited for local conditions, resulting in low productivity.
- Labor has been extremely expensive. Some categories of skilled labor have been in short supply. Growing government intolerance of immigrant labor and crackdowns on illegal residents are further complicating this problem.
- Lack of managerial experience and expertise, particularly at the middle-management level, with little likelihood of remedying this problem. Many Kuwaitis prefer the security of public sector jobs. Individuals who are highly trained have no interest in middle-management positions.
- Complicated customs procedures. These have resulted in delays in the delivery of imported raw materials and spare parts.
- Chronic shortages of electricity and water supplies. There are occasional power failures.
- Limited access of private sector companies to the capital market, made worse by the growing strictness

of the authorities in the aftermath of the Manakh crash, and by the reticence of investors about buying shares.

All of these factors have contributed to low productivity and the slow growth of the industrial sector. The major problem, namely the small domestic market, could be offset by successful economic integration among GCC countries, who have already eliminated customs duties on manufactured goods among themselves. This could substantially expand the market for Kuwaiti products, although it opens the door to competition from other GCC countries.

The major weakness of the industrial sector stems from Kuwait's predilection for trade, as evidenced by the rapid growth of the service sector. The government appears to have grown increasingly disenchanted with the manufacturing sector, and is assigning it a relatively low priority. Having concluded that there is little hope for serious diversification of the economy through industrialization, the government seems to be focusing its concern on the financial sector, its support to the industrial sector being largely limited at present to the assistance provided by the partly government-owned Industrial Bank of Kuwait.

5.4 INDUSTRIAL BANK OF KUWAIT (IBK). The Industrial Bank of Kuwait was establishd in late 1973 and started operations in late 1974. The IBK is jointly owned by government insitutions and large commerical banks (54.48 percent by 14 Kuwaiti financial and commercial institutions, including 8.96 percent held by the National Bank of Kuwait, the rest being held by government and quasi-government institutions). Its main function is to assist in the development of private manufacturing activities. Its total capitalization has grown from KD 10 million ($35.7 million) at its inception to KD 30 million ($103.9 million) at the end of 1982.

IBK support to the industrial sector has included:

- Long-term loans at low interest (5 percent/year)
- Industrial leases at nominal rent
- Equity participation for new industries

The IBK is currently assisting in the financing of over 250 companies with varying activities, including construction materials, chemicals, food and beverages, textiles, metal products, furniture, and paper. Its most recent annual report highlights its predilection for import substitutes, and eventually for high-technology industries. It is a part owner of three Kuwaiti financial institutions, as well as two foreign-based ones.

During the first five months of 1983, the Industrial Bank of Kuwait reported the approval of 19 loans totalling KD 30.4 million ($103.9 million) (compared to KD 25 million ($86.6 million) for the same period the year before), with IBK providing KD 15.9 million ($54.4 million) (compared with KD 11.7 million ($40.5 million) for the same period the year before). Its total financing is believed to have been in excess of the KD 28.8 million ($99.8 million) approved at the end of 1982.

Although partly government-owned, the IBK is largely autonomous and in many ways represents the interests of the non-oil mannufacturing sector to the government. Its management has echoed private sector complaints about government indiffence to non-oil manufacturing development and the lack of a coordinated government strategy for the development of the sector.

In April 1983, IBK was instrumental in setting up the Industrial Investing Company (of which it owns 21 percent, as does the government; the Public Institution for Social Security accounts for 10 percent, and a number of private and semi-private financial institutions for the rest). The company is to carry out all investment finance and trade operations, and to administer industrial projects.

5.5 INDUSTRIAL PRODUCTION. The range of Kuwaiti industrial products is considerable for a country of Kuwait's size, which may in fact reflect the lack of a coordinated government-strategy for industrial development. Chemical industries (excluding petrochemicals) declined in relative importance during the seventies, growing at a mere 0.69 percent annually during the period 1974-80 (the average being 16.28 percent for the manufacturing sector). They now account for 20 percent of non-petrochemical industrial production (compared to 47.6 percent in 1974). Non-metal products, which grew fastest over the same period, were the largest as a percentage of manufacturing output by the end 1980 (27.2 percent), followed by chemicals, metal products (13.5 percent), furniture and wood products (13.5 percent), food and beverages (12.4 percent), textiles and clothing (7.7 percent), and paper and printing (5.7 percent).

6.
AGRICULTURE, LIVESTOCK AND FISHERIES SECTOR

6.1 GENERAL CONDITIONS. The agricultural sector in Kuwait contributes an insignificant percentage to GDP. Since the early seventies, the percentage of agriculture in total GDP has been well under 1 percent. This sector has maintained its relative share of GDP through the petroleum expansion period largely because of government expenditure. In 1983, its contribution to GDP was 0.5 percent.

6.2 LONGSTANDING PROBLEMS. Kuwait's potential for developing its agricultural sector is limited. Although the Kuwaiti government is understandably anxious to reduce dependence on imported foodstuffs, planners intent on expanding the agricultural sector face several problems. These include:

- Very limited water resources. Annual rainfall averages 140 mm on the coast, and less than 80 mm in the interior. Occasional brief but very heavy rainfall in winter generates runoff deposits, which collect in small depressions and form shallow sand and gravel aquifers. Oases like Fahaheel, Tawil and Jahra, developed through the of extraction of water close to the surface, but the amount of water was severely limited. Groundwater, particularly the Kuwait formation at Rawdhatain, the Dammam formation near al-Ahmadi, and smaller formations at Umm Al Aish, Al Abdali, and Umm er-Radhuma, is more difficult to extract; it is often saline or brackish, and requires distillation to make it potable.
- Kuwait has turned to desalination. Work on a major plant has been commenced by Idemitsu of Japan (the Gulf oil spill does not appear to have caused irreversible damage), but desalinated water is too expensive to support agriculture economically except for experimental (greenhouse and hyrdoponic) cultivation. A project at Al-Sulaybiya produces purified water from sewage for irrigation purposes.

- Extremely high temperatures in summer (40° C or more), with frosts in winter, a high evaporation rate, and occasional sandstorms.
- Infertile soil with minimal sediments throughout the country. Slightly better (but still inferior) soil is to be found in a narrow zone south and southwest from the bay of Kuwait.
- Urban sprawl, which has preempted much of the best available agricultural land, and led to high real estate prices because of the potential for land development for construction purposes.

6.3 AGRICULTURAL PRODUCTION. Total cultivable land in 1979 was no more than 153,900 hectares (out of a total area of 1,781,800 hectares). Of these, 16,300 hectares were not utilized: only 3,600 hectares were cultivated (1,300 for vegetables and 2,300 for fruit), the rest being utilized for pasturage. Underground brackish water is the major source of irrigation. The major crops are: alfalfa (year round); tomatoes (9,000 tons produced in 1981); chard, parsley and coriander (winter); melons, mallow, basil and purslane (summer); and other fruits and vegetables, notably dates, citrus fruits, pomegranates, bananas, figs, grapes, radishes, eggplant, onions, cucumbers, squash, and garlic.

6.4 EXPERIMENTAL FARMING. Experimental farming has, in some instances, proved spectacularly successful in Kuwait – although on a small scale. There is a large experimental farm at Omariyah, operated with help from the United Nations Food and Agriculture Organization (FAO). The operation of many farming units involves the use of greenhouses, plasticulture, drip irrigation, and, perhaps most interestingly, hydroponics, a technique which requires only 10 percent of the water needed in conventional farming and is relatively capital-intensive.

6.5 LIVESTOCK AND POULTRY. The same problems facing agriculture limit the availability of pastures and grazing land. Most livestock is raised by bedouins. There were 47 cattle farms in 1981, ranging in size from 300 head to 2,000 head per farm. All such farms are privately owned, but the government provides considerable support (technical assistance, direct subsidies for meat and milk production, and veterinary services). In 1981, there were an estimated 11,000 cattle, 158,000 sheep, and 110,000 goats. There is a single large scale dairy farm, the Kuwait Dairy (1,500 cattle), but there are plans to set up a sheep raising center of 1,100 acres at Sulaybiya, west of Kuwait City, to be fed by alfalfa grown on 925 hectares irrigated with water from the nearby water purification plant.

Limited poultry production (500 - 600 broilers per day) and likewise limited egg production occur in a number of small farms. The estimated chicken population for 1981 was 6.2 million. The prospects for mass production of chicken meat and eggs, the requirements for which are less stringent than for other livestock, are considered quite good. The government is encouraging the development of larger farms with 51 percent government participation, in the hope of achieving self-sufficiency in chicken meat and eggs in the near future.

6.6 FISHERIES. Fishing is a traditional industry. While it has been eclipsed in importance, it meets nearly all of local demand. In 1980, the total catch was 3,000 tons. The Gulf oil slick poses a considerable threat to marine life, but the effect on fish production has yet to be determined.

The United Fisheries Company of Kuwait (jointly owned by the government and the private sector) was established in 1972; the number of vessels it operates has since risen from 90 to 150. Shrimp is its most profitable catch (averaging 3 million pounds a year). Shrimp and food processing facilities are planned; a major plant has recently opened in Shuaiba.

6.7 FOOD NEEDS. Limited capacity has led to considerable dependence on imports to meet food needs. Preliminary estimates indicate that Kuwait is totally dependent on imports to meet its needs in wheat, barley, rice (imported mostly from India), legumes, maize, cheese, and refined sugar. Imports are also needed to meet 61.7 percent of vegetable needs, 97.7 percent of fruit needs, 84.9 percent of dates, 59.9 percent of meat (imported mostly from Australia), 97.7 percent of poultry meat (imported mostly from Brazil), and 81.9 percent of eggs. In 1981, KD 204.4 million ($726.3 million) was spent on the import of food and beverages (10.5 percent of total imports). There is concern that, with a growing population, Kuwait could become increasingly dependent on foreigners for food supplies, and so especially vulnerable to a food boycott.

7. MANPOWER

7.1 THE EXPATRIATE LABOR FORCE. The manpower shortage in Kuwait is symptomatic of many development problems in the Gulf. The Gulf governments have embarked on ambitious development plans, financed by a capital intensive sector but not supported by a large population. Kuwait's population was estimated at 1.67 million in 1983 (an increase of 90,000 from 1982 or 5.6 percent per annum). While exact estimates of the foreign population are unreliable (because of illegal immigration), government sources believe 58 percent of the population was non-Kuwaiti in 1980. Out of a workforce of 492,000 in 1980, 384,000 or 78 percent were non-Kuwaiti.

As late as the 1950s, almost the entire population was indigenous. With the increase in oil revenues and consequent increase in development projects, a large, skilled labor force was needed, and Kuwait turned to expatriate workers. Foreign workers include Arabs (especially Egyptians and Palestinians), Iranians, Indians, Pakistanis, and more recently, Koreans and Filipinos. The manpower shortage is most acutely felt in the area of middle-management positions, in which few Kuwaitis seem to be interested. Consequently, a large number of middle-management positions are occupied by Palestinians, many of whom hold Jordanian passports.

A number of large industries have very few Kuwaiti employees. Al-Ghanim Industries, for instance, which is a major contracting and industrial firm, had twelve Kuwaitis in a workforce of 3,000 as recently as 1981. Only 6 percent of the employees of joint stock companies are Kuwaiti, in technical violation of industrial law, which requires that 25 percent be Kuwaiti. The banking industry tends to be dominated by Levantines, notably Palestinians; only 15 percent of its workforce is Kuwaiti.

Many of those involved in agriculture are Iranians who live in appallingly primitive dwellings. Koreans predominate in the construction industry because South Koreans work for construction firms abroad in lieu of part of their military service; this circumstance makes them less volatile than other foreign workers, as evidenced by the fact that many of them live in tents.

Statistics on labor permits issued in 1982 (the last year for which statistics are available) indicate that construction continues to attract the most foreigners; it accounted for 49.3 percent of all new permits issued to the 68,799 foreign workers entering Kuwait for the first time. The service industries (wholesale and retail trade, restaurants and hotels) followed construction and accounted for 20.2 percent of new permits. Next came general and social services (9.4 percent), manufacturing (8.4 percent) and transport, storage and communications (6.4 percent). Other sectors (mining, finance and agriculture) accounted for the remaining 6.3 percent. These figures do not include illegal workers, who are especially numerous in the service industries.

The 1982 figures indicate the growth in the percentage of non-Arab Asian workers. Asian nationals (including Indians, Pakistanis, Bengalis, Koreans and Filipinos) formed an estimated 15 percent of Kuwait's population in 1980, compared to Arab groups who constituted 42 percent). But Asians received 53.3 percent of all work permits issued in 1982, while Arabs received 42.8 percent. Europeans and Americans received a mere 3.9 percent. Of illegal immigrants, who are not included in these figures, Arabs are probably the most numerous.

7.2 RESTRICTIONS ON NON-CITIZENS AND WOMEN. Kuwaiti law draws sharp distincion between Kuwaiti citizens and non-Kuwaitis. Only citizens can own real estate and obtain import licenses; Kuwaitis must be involved in all businesses and contracts. These requirements have encouraged Kuwaitis to become silent partners in various commercial enterprises, allowing foreign partners to manage the firms once the firms have been jointly established.The number of silent partnerships has increased in spite of the central training institutes established by the government to prepare Kuwaitis for jobs currently held by foreigners. Although the law does not discriminate against women in employment, only about 12 percent of the labor force are women, and only 2.5 percent are Kuwaiti women. Kuwait is somewhat more tolerant of women participating in the workforce than many other Gulf countries. A number of industries – for example, the Kuwait Electric Wiring Accessories Company – employ women in their factories, an unheard of phenomenon in many Gulf states.

The high percentage of foreigners in the workforce has alarmed Kuwaiti planners, who as recently as 1981, projected a rapid increase in the non-Kuwaiti population to as many as 1.22 million in 1985 (compared to 805,000 in 1980), while the Kuwaiti population was expected to rise modestly to 682,000 in 1985 (compared to 569,000 in 1980). The estimate of growth of the foreign population is now regarded as excessive, in view of the prevailing recession which has meant shrinking opportunities for foreigners in most sectors of the Kuwaiti economy. Nonetheless, the planners are still believed to be concerned about the large (and still growing) foreign presence.

As a result of the planners' concern, and also because of the overall slowdown in the Kuwaiti economy (reflected in negative growth), the following two additional restrictions were placed on the employment of foreigners in 1983:

- Work permits issued to non-Kuwaitis engaged by the private sector are henceforth renewable every two years.
- Residency laws have been amended to make it impossible for expatriates working without valid permits and government employees with terminated contracts to move to the private sector without first leaving the country and applying for permits from abroad.

Nonetheless, the Kuwaiti economy continued to attract foreign workers in 1983. During the first quarter of 1983, the last period for which statistics were available, new entrants totalled 21,760, as compared to 20,357 for the same period in 1982. At the same time, only 3,620 foreigners departed from Kuwait, a considerable decline from the figure of 6,205 during the first quarter of 1982.

7.3 SOCIAL WELFARE AND POPULATION. Development projects have placed great emphasis on public health and education. The death rate has been significantly lowered (5 per 1,000 in 1980) without a corresponding drop in the fertility rate (207 per 1,000 in 1980). As mentioned previously, the total population is expected to increase rapidly in the near future as in the past (the growth rate was nearly 6 percent annually during the seventies). Because of continued legal and illegal immigration, however, the percentage of foreigners in the population is likely to continue to rise.

Foreigners are not offered the same range of social services as are available to Kuwaitis. The outgoing Finance Minister, Abd al-Latif al-Hamad, was believed to favor a reduction in the range of those services which are offered free of charge, in effect reducing the benefits of Kuwaiti citizenship. This would have made possible the naturalization of a larger number of foreigners (it is now next to impossible for a foreigner to be naturalized), making Kuwait more socially balanced. His resignation last year was taken as an indication that such a policy will probably not be implemented – at any rate, not at a speed that could bring about a dramatic social transformation.

7.4 EMPLOYMENT PATTERNS. In 1982, the largest percentage (64 percent) of the labor force was employed in the services sector, and nearly three quarters of these were government employed. Non-Kuwaitis make up the bulk of the industrial force. Kuwaitis now form 22 percent of the private workforce according to some estimates, against 12 percent in 1975. One of Kuwait's less visible problems is the large number of workers employed by the government. The public sector, which absorbs 3,000 new employees every year, is considered overstaffed; in 1979 it is estimated that the government employed 65,000 "unnecessary" functionaries. Kuwaitis seem to favor government employment, so much so that less than one-quarter of employed Kuwaitis were in the private sector in the mid-1970s. To encourage Kuwaitis to leave government service for the private sector, which actually pays much better than the government, the government in 1975 granted a government pension to all Kuwaitis regardless of their employers.

About one-half of government employees are foreign, mainly Egyptian and Palestinian. Many of these enjoy considerable influence in government circles, but their general socio-economic status is below that of native Kuwaitis.

7.5 PROJECTIONS. While there are many imponderables that could affect population and employment patterns in the future, the following developments are deemed highly likely:

- Total population will continue to expand, reflecting low mortality, continued high fertility, and a high influx of immigrants, approaching 2 million around 1990.
- The percentage of foreigners will almost certainly not diminish, despite growing government intolerance toward immigration. The limited availability of new opportunities, and the entry into the workforce of educated Kuwaitis will at least slow down its growth.

- The percentage of Asians relative to other expatriates (especially Arabs) will continue to rise, reflecting a tacit policy of discouraging Arabs, whose presence is deemed politically explosive. It should be noted, however, that Kuwait has handled its Arab population fairly well and is viewed as a second home by many Palestinians, who are active participants in the country's cultural life (especially in the press), even though they do not hold citizenship.
- The percentage of Americans and Europeans will continue to be low and probably diminish. Kuwait has been less inclined to fill top management position with Europeans and Americans than other nearby Gulf states.
- The resurgence of Islamic fundamentalism as a consequence of the Iranian revolution, as well as a closer relationship with Saudi Arabia in the context of GCC cooperation, have led to the development of a mood of social conservatism, making it unlikely that women will have many new opportunities in the labor market.
- The benefits of citizenship will almost certainly continue to be impressive; naturalization is an unlikely prospect for long-time foreign residents of Kuwait who are desirous of citizenship (many of them Palestinians born in Kuwait who have lived in no other country).

8. CONSTRUCTION

8.1 GENERAL CONDITIONS In the early years of Kuwait's development, the construction sector was a significant proportion of GDP (10 percent). By the end of the seventies a considerable part of the infrastructure and residential housing had been built, so that the value-added of the construction industry had declined to its present (1983) level of 4.6 percent of GDP. The fortunes of the construction sector have declined further due to:

- The financial crash of 1982, which has seriously hurt the the construction sector. Many private-sector projects with a large allocation for construction were financed through borrowing, and the shake-up of the credit market led to the collapse, abandonment,or postponement of such projects. Worse yet, many major debtors were obliged to dump their real estate holdings on an already weak market.
- The mood of fiscal conservatism which was most pronounced during the tenure of the outgoing Finance Minister,Abd al-Latif al-Hamad, and which continues to prevail to a large extent as a result of shrinking oil revenues. This has led to the postponement or cancellation of several government projects which would have yielded revenue for major contractors. Among these is the waterfront project, which had been planned in six phases. Phase 1 is being implemented at KD 38 million ($130 million), phases 2 and 3 are being sharply curtailed, and phases 4 and 5 are being combined.
- The sharp fall in transit trade because of the Iraq-Iran war, which eliminates the need for major expansion of port facilities for the time being at least. As a result, the Shuwaikh port expansion project has been shelved. This would have entailed the construction of 22 additional berths at the cost of KD 200-250 million ($683.6-854.5 million), a figure already cut back by Associated Marine Consultants of the Netherlands.

- The crackdown on illegal residents has hit construction especially hard. Illegal residents were a major fixture of the construction sector; their gradual elimination has led to escalating costs.
- The slack in business activity is delaying projects geared toward retail facility construction, as an excess supply is developing in commercial buildings.

At the same time, there are several positive factors in the construction market, namely:

- In spite of government austerity, the 1983-84 allocation for developmental expenditure (KD 622 million [$2.126 billion]) is about the same amount allocated two years ago, indicating the government's commitment to infrastructural development and maintenance. Furthermore, the 1984-85 budget projects an increase of nearly 30 percent in expenditure on development projects.
- In the first quarter of 1983, 212 permits were issued for public sector construction, a 29 percent increase from the year-end figure. There was a large increase in residential construction in early 1983.
- Real estate prices recovered somewhat in the first half of 1983.
- With the settlement of post-dated checks largely completed, and compensation paid by the government, the liquidity position of many investors has improved. This is particularly true of those designated as "small investors," for whom relief in the form of cash payments or bonds redeemable at a discount has been made available through the Small Investors Relief Fund.
- A recent government decision to award contracts to Kuwaiti firms whenever possible, and to require foreign construction firms to subcontract more work to local companies, is expected to ease the pressure on Kuwaiti construction firms.
- Rental laws permit rent increases of up to 100 percent after the elapse of a five-year period, making residential property potentially profitable.
- The massive construction undertaken in recent years requires considerable maintenance, repair and upgrading, which the government is committed to providing in the case of public buildings.
- The excess supply of funds following the financial crash is expected by some to find its way to the real estate market due to the lack of alternative investment opportunities. However, many are fearful

that much of the money could be channelled abroad instead.

- The government land acquisition program, primarily intended as a form of wealth transfer at its inception, is being used by the government to firm up real estate prices. In January 1983, KD 150 million ($512.7 million) from the general reserves was added to the KD 300 million ($1.025 billion) allocation for land acquisitions in the 1982-83 budget.

8.2 TYPES OF CONSTRUCTION. The types of construction have closely followed the economic development of Kuwait. In the fifties and sixties most construction was of medical facilities, housing, infrastructure, and oil facilities. (The Kuwaiti government provides a home for each citizen.) After that time the emphasis shifted to industrial facilities.

Funds for new projects have been severely limited, but new construction is taking place and contracts are being awarded. Contracting procedures have become more complex; there is a clear attempt to provide local firms with as much assistance as possible, which implies a bias against foreign contractors. There is still an interest in building retail outlets, residential housing, and government complexes (known as "district centers"). These are intended to serve as community centers for localities outside of Kuwait city. They provide communal institutions (theaters, libraries, mosques), as well as facilities for retailers and government agencies in a compact, climate-controlled environment and allow for better civic planning. Plans have been completed for the development of such centers in Hawalli, Salmiya and Fahaheel. There is also an ambitious plan for a development of the Fintas district center (primarily for retail purposes) at an estimated cost of $1.2 billion.

Other areas in which demand for construction is considerable include public housing, road construction (undertaken by the Ministry of Public Works), and electric generators and desalination plants (built by the Electricity and Water Ministry).

8.3 HOUSING. Housing is a major priority. The National Housing Authority is charged with the provision of housing for all Kuwaiti citizens, who are entitled to low-cost housing as a citizenship right.

The NHA was founded in 1974 to cope with the increasing number of applications for government housing which had previously been handled by the Ministry of Work and Social Affairs. Initially the NHA was supposed to handle the housing requirements of the low-income group (LIG = citizens with an income lower than $860 per month), while the Housing Ministry, formed in 1975, was supposed to handle all other applications. The scope of activities of the NHA was subsequently enlarged to comprise the average-income group (AIG – with a monthly salary of $860-$1,725), and the relocation of rural inhabitants (mostly nomadic bedouins) into sedentary habitations. This accounts for the growth of the NHA's budget for its past (1975-80) five-year plan to KD 607 million.

During the period 1975-80, 16,000 houses and apartments were completed, nearly two thirds of which were government houses for bedouins, the bulk of the remainder going to the LIG. A total of 8,000 houses projected in that plan are still under construction, most of which are for the LIG. At the end of the first plan, nearly 35,000 families were still waiting to receive housing through the program, while nearly 12,000 new applicants were being added to the waiting list every year.

The second five-year plan (1981-86) of the NHA aims at providing housing for 280,000 Kuwaiti citizens through the building of 36,000 housing units, for which 3,130 hectares have been allocated. A large percentage of the projected units are for the LIG families, many of whose dwellings are to be built in the Fneitiss and South Sabah Al-Salem Greater Area, West Aghaila, Ardiya, Jahra and Fintas. In June 1980, an additional KD 870 million (nearly $3 billion) was allocated to the NHA, increasing the total amount to be spent of housing from 1974-85 to KD 1.364 billion ($4.7 billion).

The priorities and policies of the NHA have been clearly outlined. Priority is being given to the human element over functional (e.g. traffic-oriented) projects. The LIG still receives the bulk of the housing. The type of housing was standardized to consist of two-storey villas in early 1983. Stricter procedures have been introduced in tendering to insure higher quality, while local contractors were promised 80 percent of total projects in 1981.

The NHA's backlog, currently estimated at about 30,000 applicants, is expected to remain high as the Kuwaiti population continues to grow. The current backlog should be met over the next five years, but a surge in demand due to the booming population is expected shortly thereafter.

8.4 WORKERS. Ninety-five percent of the construction labor force is non-Kuwaiti; only 2 percent of Kuwaiti workers are in construction. Nearly half of all new (legal) entrants in 1982 were employed in the construction sector. But the high proportion of foreigners in construction is not considered to be one of the high-risk areas of social instability usually associated with large expatriate populations. Since construction workers are generally at a low skill level, they can be replaced, and therefore dispersed, relatively easily. Furthermore, many construction workers are Asian, especially Korean, and these historically have been docile.

9.
FINANCIAL SECTOR.

9.1 EVALUATION. Kuwait's financial sector (which accounted for 4.8 percent of GDP at current prices in 1983) has grown rapidly in recent years. The financial sector's contribution to GDP registered a 27.9 percent growth rate in 1981 and a 24.8 percent growth rate in 1982, despite the Manakh crash, which threatened to destabilize domestic credit. In 1983, the growth of the financial sector slowed to 11.1 percent. While critics have pointed out that the sector's robustness is predicated on government support, it must be said that such support has waned in recent years as the government, and particularly the Finance Ministry, have seemed to favor discipline over rapid growth.

In 1983, for instance, government deposits declined 8 percent KD 1.094 billion ($3.789 billion) from KD 1.189 billion ($4.118.5 billion) in 1982, straining one of the main sources of liquidity in the economy. The money supply was permitted to grow a mere 4.4 percent. The interest rates on 7-day Central Bank bills were raised sharply in early 1983 (after having been lowered in late 1982) from 2.75 percent to 4.00 percent, while the interest rate on 91 day bills was raised from 5.50 percent to 5.688 percent. By the end of 1983, the seasonally adjusted figure for money showed a 5.3 percent decline.

The effect has been to limit liquidity and narrow the scope of action for the country's financial institutions. Not surprisingly, the monthly average for bank clearings was drastically lower in 1983 (67.2 percent), having climbed steadily in previous years and having nearly doubled in 1982. While claims on the private sector continued their steady growth, bank reserves have eroded substantially; they registered a 40.5 percent decline at the end of 1983 compared to the same period a year earlier. The effect of this erosion of the monetary base on the supply of domestic liquidity can be imagined.

9.2 AFTER MANAKH. Although the main indicators do not encourage optimism about the health of the financial sector, the government has made attempts to stabilize the market in the aftermath of the Manakh crash. These have taken the following forms:

- The government has purchased shares on the stock market to shore up prices through the two government-controlled investment companies. Estimates of spending on this activity stood at KD 250 million ($854.5 million) for the first five months of 1983, and is believed to have totalled KD 750 million ($2,563 million) to date (as of mid-1984).
- The allocation for land acquisitions, a traditional means of injecting liquidity into the financial system, was increased at mid-point in the 1982-83 budget by KD 150 million ($512.7 million). This has also provided support to the related real estate market.
- The injection of additional funds through the Small Investors Relief Fund. This provides cash payments or bonds discountable with banks to small investors hurt by the Manakh crash. A total of KD 3 billion ($10.3 billion) is estimated to have been disbursed by this Fund so far.
- The government has indicated that, while it is determined to maintain discipline, under no account will it permit a collapse of any of the commercial banks.

This has prevented the financial system from sustaining more damage than some anticipated in the aftermath of the Manakh crash. While the departure late last year of the Finance Minister, Abd al-Latif al-Hamad gave an impression of instability at the top, this was quickly dispelled; many in the financial community were not displeased by the change of leadership, the outgoing Minister having been accused of inflexibility in dealing with the crisis and a determination to implement fiscal austerity in the face of the deepening recession. Al-Hamad's successor, Shaikh Ali, has shown himself to be pragmatic and possessing of keen political sense; he has delayed the proposed increase in electricity and water charges, and is a firm proponent of fiscal stimulation (a fact mirrored in the proposed budget), which indicates that he is less austerity-minded than his predecessor. While such behavior has been attacked by many (notably outside Kuwait) as irresponsible in the long-run, there is little doubt that his flexibility and expansionary outlook have done much to prevent business confidence inside Kuwait from collapsing altogether.

There are some positive signs in the financial sector. The international KD bond market was reopened with a UBK bond issue in mid-1983. Then the domestic Kuwait bond market was reopened in late 1983 with a KFTCIC bond issue. The local syndicated market also rallied with the setting up of an NBK-managed loan for a major business figure at around the same time. The stock market, however, remains depressed. Most stock values are well below their 1982 peak – primarily a reflection of the uncertainty engendered by the Gulf War (which has placed in jeopardy the operations of many firms listed on the stock exchange).

The major aspects of the postdated check problem were settled early this year, restoring some measure of confidence and making additional liquidity available. Nonetheless, pending litigation and bankruptcy proceedings insure that the after-effects of the crisis will continue to be felt by the financial community.

9.3 COMMERCIAL BANKS. The banking sector is tightly controlled in Kuwait. Only six commercial banks (as opposed to specialized and investment banks) are permitted to operate, and it seems inconceivable that the number could be increased in the future. No foreign competition of any kind is permitted, unlike in neighboring UAE and Bahrain where foreign banks are permitted to open branches.

This has resulted in the existing banks being fairly sturdy, although the Manakh collapse did shake them, as it did everyone else in the financial sector. Strict domestic control of commercial banking activity (particularly in the area of loan syndication) has prompted the development of largely Kuwaiti-owned foreign-based commercial banks competing for the offshore Kuwaiti commercial banking market. Foremost among these is the Bahrain-based Arab Banking Corporation.

The largest (in terms of assets) and probably most robust domestically-based Kuwaiti bank is the National Bank of Kuwait, with assets totalling KD 2.647 billion ($9.0 billion), and an income of KD 23 million ($78.6 million) at the end of 1983. Gulf Bank and the Commercial Bank of Kuwait have nearly always been tied for second place (the latter's assets totalled KD 1.917 billion [$6.6 billion], and its income KD 16.3 million [$55.71 million] at the end of 1983). Al-Ahli Bank usually follows, followed in turn by the Bank of Kuwait and the Middle East (assets were KD 1.205 billion [$4.1 billion] and income KD 7.5 million [$25.6 million]). Burgan Bank is ranked last (assets KD 686 million [$2.335 billion], income KD 5.1 million [$17.4 million] at the end of 1983).

The commercial banking community as a whole, although badly shaken by the Manakh crisis, appears to have weathered the storm. While a Central Bank ban on the discounting of postdated checks had prevented the banks from being too deeply involved in a loose credit market that was doomed to collapse, a number of banks suffered losses as many of their customers were forced to declare bankruptcy (the banks having had no effective mechanism of determining credit-worthiness prior to the Manakh crash), domestic liquidity declined, and the monetary authorities tightened their control of the economy. Another complication is that even now it is next to impossible to determine the exact net worth of many bank customers, the settlement of post-dated check obligations being far less final than the government perceives it to be.

The 1983 figures show changes in banking conditions largely as a result of the crisis. While commercial bank claims on the private sector continued their expansion (they grew 10.7 percent in 1983), as did their foreign assets (which grew 2.2 percent in 1983), KD loans and overdrafts to both residents and non-residents were reduced, releasing some liquidity. Banks divested some of their holdings of Central Bank bills (which fell from KD 469.7 million [$1.605 billion] to KD 276.1 million [$943.7 million] in the course of the year), switching instead to the higher-yielding Relief Bonds issued by the the government. As a result of this and of the fall in bank balances with the Central Bank, bank reserves declined by 40.5 percent in 1983. The percentage of assets invested abroad fell slightly to 23 percent (from 25 percent in 1982).

On the liability side, government deposits at commercial banks fell (8 percent) in 1983, as did sight deposits (which fell 7.7 percent), reflecting a shifting rate structure. Time deposits, which are the major source of funds for banks, registered an increase of 8.4 percent.

The interbank rates (the rates at which banks lend to each other) fluctuated in the course of the year. The most significant of these, the overnight rate which generally reflects the availability of liquidity in the banking system, rose on a monthly average basis during the first three quarters of the year (from 2.52 percent during the last quarter of 1982 to 6.31 percent during the third quarter of 1983). It fell considerably during the last quarter of 1983 (to 4.23) reflecting increased bank liquidity. All other interbank rates behaved differently; the longer-term rates tended to decline in the course of the year, while the shorter-term rates tended to increase.

9.4 OTHER FINANCIAL INSTITUTIONS. Other financial institutions in Kuwait comprise investment companies and specialized banks. They are significantly smaller than commercial banks (their foreign assets totalled KD 1.095 billion [$3.743 billion] at the end of 1982, against foreign assets of KD 2.445 billion [$8.5 billion] for commercial banks).

Investment companies are actively involved in buying and selling financial securities, as well as underwriting and syndicating loans and, in many instances, real estate acquisitions. Investment company portfolios are biased toward short-term investments, although they have made attempts to extend the maturities of their investments by attracting longer-term funds and establishing a Kuwaiti CD market. The major investment companies, known as the "three Ks," comprise:

- Kuwait Investment Company, the oldest Arab bond house. It was founded in 1961, and since then has been actively engaged in trading and underwriting. Through the period 1979-83, it was either the first or second-ranked Arab institution in every activity it undertook. Furthermore, it has continually dominated the floating rate sector (the issue of floating rate notes or FRNs). Its international bond market activities were valued at $494.21 million in 1982, a record year. Of this total, 49.8 percent was accounted for by "straight" (non-floating) dollar financing, 28.8 percent by dollar FRNs, 6.5 percent by KD financing. Figures are not available for all of 1983, but the January-June estimates for total activities ($93,99 million) indicate a decline.
- Kuwait International Investment Company, the youngest of the three Ks, was founded in 1983. It is involved in real estate and investment banking activities. Its activities in the international bond market peaked in 1981, when they totalled $371.97 million of which $151.01 million was for bond issues in other currencies than U.S. dollars (which accounted for 13.8 percent of total) or KD (which accounted for 15.7 percent of total). Its activities shrank substantially in 1982, totalling $93.33 million but the figures for January-June ($73.81 million) indicate an improvement. By the end of 1983, total assets had increased from KD 181.9 million ($621.7 million) in 1982 to KD 211.5 million ($722.9 million), while net income had fallen sharply to KD 3.1 million ($10.6 million) from KD 8.5 million (29.0 million).

– Kuwait Foreign Trading, Contracting and Investment Company, was founded in 1965. It is now 80 percent government-owned. Its activities encompass the international bond market and the international market for syndicated loans. The level of its activities in the international bond markets has fluctuated. It stood at $233.52 million in 1982, 35.3 percent of which was in KD bond financing. January-June 1983 figures ($54.74 million) indicate a declining involvement in the international bond market. In the international syndicated loan market, KFTCIC activities peaked in 1981, when they underwrote $806.84 million in loans. The figure dropped to $430.02 million in 1982, and stood at $249.84 million for January – June 1983. KFTCIC seems to favor loans for industrial and development projects, and particularly in other Arab countries, in whose behalf an estimated 31.5 percent of all KFTCIC loans have been underwritten so far. By the end of 1983, total KFTCIC assets stood at KD 919.3 million ($3.142 billion) (an increase from KD 787.1 million [$2.726 billion] in 1982), while net income had dropped sharply from KD 9.8 million ($33.9 million) to KD 4.8 million ($16.4 million). KFTCIC was instrumental in implementing government intervention in the domestic stock market last year.

The major specialized banks include the Savings and Credit Bank, which was established in 1965 and had an authorized capital of KD 1 billion ($3.5 billion) in November 1982; the Kuwait Real Estate Bank, with assets totalling KD 655.2 million ($2.269 billion) and net income totalling KD 7 million ($23.9 million) in 1983; the Kuwait Finance House, an Islamic banking institution, 51 percent privately held, and growing very fast (61 percent deposit growth and 84 percent net profit growth in 1982); and the Industrial Bank of Kuwait.

9.5 THE STOCK MARKET. The Kuwait stock market has played a major role in the development of the financial sector but unfortunately not a positive one.

The first price decline in the market occurred in December, 1977. The government responded by intervening (in April 1978) and buying KD 150 million ($551.9 million) worth of shares. The nominal value of stocks was simultaneously reduced, increasing the number of shares on the market. The government did not, however, resell the shares it had purchased, so that the burgeoning demand (in response to phenomenal capital gains witnessed especially in 1979-80) was frustrated.

This led to the development, in 1981, of a parallel stock market known as "al-Manakh." That market was totally unregulated; "Gulf" shares (of companies supposedly based outside Kuwait) were on it. Enormous profits were realized through sheer speculation; some of the companies whose shares were being traded did not even exist. This increased the demand for credit, and when the hard-pressed banks refused to accommodate creditors, they bypassed the system by issuing postdated checks, on which the premium steadily climbed (in anticipation of profits) to 300 percent. The amount of credit thus dispensed reached a massive KD 27 billion ($95.9 billion). When it became apparent (by the late summer of 1982) that the government was not going to intervene this time to save speculators, the market crashed.

Kuwait has never quite recovered from the impact of that crash. Bankruptcies proliferated; financial institutions were shaken; real estate prices plummeted; and liquidity was sharply curtailed. It took over a year of haggling (in the National Assembly and elsewhere) before a formula was worked out, reducing the premiums on checks to 25 percent.

The government has since sought to alleviate the effect of the crisis through relief assistance to small investors who were hurt, for whose benefit the Small Investors Relief Fund was set up to disburse cash payment of up to KD 100,000 ($346,380) per investor holding claims of up to KD 2 million ($6.9 million). In addition, payments were made in bonds discountable at 7.5 percent with the banks.

In an effort to impose discipline on share trading, the government has formally constituted the official stock market (which has had official status since 1982) as the Kuwait Securities Market last year, to be administered by an 11-man committee (under the chairmanship of the Ministry of Commerce). While initially shares of Gulf offshore companies (traded on the parallel market) were excluded, there are indications that the government is now encouraging their official listing.

The long-term effect of the crisis on the stock market is yet to be determined. Optimists have noted that the All Kuwaiti Share Index declined by only 13 percent between end-June 1982 (before the crisis) and end-April 1983. The volume share has been subdued, if not exactly depressed – KD 650 million ($2.222 billion) worth of shares were bought from October 1982 to mid-June 1983; of these KD 250 million ($854.5 million) worth were bought in the first five months of 1983. In mid-1984, the condition of the stock market remained unencouraging, with most stock prices well below their pre-crisis levels and the volume of stocks traded relatively low.

9.6 KD BOND MARKET. The other capital market in Kuwait, the KD bond market, has also undergone varied experiences. It was first tapped as early as 1968, when the World Bank and other international agencies made seven private placements totalling KD 135 million ($482.0 million). In 1974, legislation was passed to permit the setting up of a KD bond market. It continued to operate through November 1979, when a moratorium on new issues was imposed to alleviate the shortage of domestic liquidity. The moratorium was temporarily suspended but re-imposed in 1980. During the period 1974-80, 60 bond issues had been made, totalling more than KD 400 million ($1.474 billion).

The market was reopened in July, 1981. A moratorium was imposed in the second half of 1982 in the shadow of the Manakh crisis and diminishing liquidity. During that period, prices firmed up somewhat in spite of low liquidity, as the aggregate volume of bonds declined through bond maturation, and there continued to be a considerable positive margin on KD bonds over the cost of funding.

The domestic KD bond market was effectively reopened with a bond issue in 1983 (half fixed-rate and half floating-rate), followed by a KD 14 million ($47.9 million) two-tranche bond-offering by KFTCIC in late November 1983. As they were both accorded a good reception, most observers expected the market to revive, in line with the current revival of the local syndicated bond market.

9.7 REGULATING AUTHORITIES. The major entities in charge of determination and implementation of fiscal and monetary policy are the Central Bank and the Finance Ministry. The Central Bank is technically the more powerful of the two; it has control over the money supply and credit, and holds $6 billion of international reserves.

The Central Bank did not act energetically to contain the credit explosion which preceded the Manakh crisis. The Central Bank Governor, Hamza Abbas Husain has been accused by some of adopting drastic (if inevitable) measures to prevent bank discounting of postdated checks after having done little to place limits on the credit explosion in the preceding months. His action indicated that the government would not indefinitely accommodate speculators by allowing the volume of credit to expand; it jolted investor confidence and hastened the arrival of the day of reckoning.

Abbas Husain proved unpopular with the public because of his refusal to come to the rescue of stock market dealers. He resigned his position in October, 1983, to be replaced by Abd al-Wahab al-Tammar who, as chairman of the Kuwait Foreign Trading, Contracting and Investment Company (largely government owned) and Arab Banking Corporation (private), has excellent contacts with the financial community.

Fiscal policy is the domain of the Finance Ministry. Under the tenure of the outgoing Finance Minister,Abd al-Latif al-Hamad, the emphasis was on conservatism and economic "rationalization." Al-Hamad, considered a voice of reason, was also a vital link with the international financial community, which regretted his departure in late 1983. His successor has put into action a rescue plan for Manakh investors and adopted a pragmatic approach, which suggests that the future of the rationalization policy may be in doubt.

10.
INTERNATIONAL TRANSACTIONS

10.1 MERCHANDISE EXPORTS. The value of Kuwait's exports reached its highest level in 1980, when it stood at KD 5.569 billion ($20.53 billion) in the aftermath of the oil price hike of 1979-80. Exports fell to KD 4.446 billion ($16.388 billion) as oil revenue declined in 1981, and fell again in 1982 to KD 3.121 billion ($10.810 billion).

Kuwait's exports stood at an estimated KD 3.239 billion ($11.071 billion) in 1983, a modest (3.8 percent) increase over the previous year's record. This reflected a considerable increase in the value of oil exports, which rose 8.5 percent to KD 2.757 billion ($9.424 billion) from the previous year's level of KD 2.541 billion ($8.802 billion). This occurred in spite of the fall in oil prices, particularly in the early part of 1983, as a result of the increase in the volume of oil exports.

Kuwait's exports continue to be dominated by oil, which accounted for 85.1 percent of total exports in 1983. As a result, Kuwaiti exports have tended to be affected by fluctuations in the international oil market, registering large increases when the oil prices increased (as in 1979), and declining precipitously when oil prices fell in 1981).

Two things should, however, be noted:

- Unlike many other oil producers, Kuwait is not a revenue maximizer where oil is concerned. In other words, it does not necessarily seek to expand oil sales when oil prices are high, or to curtail oil production sharply when oil prices are low. As a result, the volume of Kuwait's exports is determined as much by Kuwaiti planners as by international fluctuations, so that oil exports rose very modestly (and total exports actually fell) in 1980, a good year for oil exporters, and also increased in 1983, a disastrous year for many OPEC producers.
- Kuwait has been successful in increasing the proportion of refined oil exports out of total oil exports, in the context of consolidating the downstream

operations of its oil industry. As the price of refined oil products is less sensitive to fluctuations in crude prices, this has generally reduced the dependence of total export value on market conditions for crude. In 1982, for instance, when the quantum of exported crude fell sharply (by 55 percent), the volume of exported refined oil products rose (by 38 percent), mitigating the decline in the total volume of oil exports. In the third quarter of 1983, the volume of refined oil exports had increased 83 percent over the same period of the previous year, while the volume of exports of crude oil fell by 48 percent, LPG by 55 percent, and crude price tumbled by 9 percent.

Kuwait's non-oil exports have been growing steadily, if slowly, in nominal terms in recent years, reflecting modest progress in economic diversification. In 1981, the last year for which detailed official statistics are available, these were dominated by manufactured goods of various types, which amounted to KD 239 million ($849.2 million), and constituted 42 percent of total non-oil exports (5.3 percent of total exports). They were followed by machinery and transport equipment (KD 223 million [$828.0 million]), and food and live animals (KD 43 million [$152.8 million], which includes re-exports). Other non-oil export items include chemicals, crude materials other than oil, beverages and tobacco.

A major factor in Kuwait's non-oil export trade is the predominance of re-exports, a circumstance which dates back to the years prior to the oil revolution, when transit trade was a major source of revenue. At present, much of Kuwait's re-export market has been shaken by the Iraq-Iran war, which poses a major threat to Gulf shipping. Kuwaiti vessels have sustained more physical damage than those of any other country, three having been hit thus far. At the same time, Iraq's inability to import goods directly has caused it to rely more heavily on the overland route from Kuwait for a major portion of its imports, some of the trade thus channeled being in defense equipment.

Asian countries absorb more than half of Kuwait's exports; as a group they imported 58 percent of Kuwait's total 1981 exports. Japan is the most important single purchaser of Kuwaiti exports (mostly oil); it accounted for 24 percent of the total in 1981. The European countries followed (18 percent of exports); the percentage may already have increased, and is likely to increase as Kuwait succeeds in selling more of its refined products in

European markets through newly-acquired European distributors.

Kuwait's export sales to all Arab countries combined are a mere 14 percent of total. Of the Arab countries, Iraq is by far the most important, its imports from Kuwait having increased phenomenally (they nearly doubled from 1980 to 1981) as a result of Iraq's limited access to sources of supply due to the war with Iran. Saudi Arabia is the second largest Arab purchaser of Kuwaiti exports; ties between the two countries are reported to be warming up.

The United States is of negligible importance as a purchaser of Kuwaiti exports, but it may find itself importing more from Kuwait if the Kuwaitis succeed in establishing a foothold in the market for refined oil products in the United States.

10.2 IMPORTS. Kuwait's imports have been growing rapidly in the past few years on account of the country's growing population, the inability of industrial production to meet the growing demand, the need for raw materials, machinery and spare parts for industrial development, the availability of foreign exchange, Kuwait's role as a re-export center (particularly to Iraq) so that some imports are channeled to other countries, and the traditional importance of trade as activity for some of Kuwait's most prominent families.

In 1982, the last year for which confirmed official statistics are available, imports are estimated to have risen to KD 2.326 billion ($8.056 billion), a 19.1 percent increase over the previous year's figure. Official estimates indicate that imports have nearly tripled over the period 1975-81, having grown at an average annual rate of 30 percent in nominal terms.

Machinery and transport equipment, which include capital goods and spare parts, are by the far the largest imports, accounting for 41 percent of total value in 1981. They are followed by manufactured goods, which accounted for 38 percent, and food and live animals, which accounted for 13 percent. Statistics for the first quarter of 1982 indicate a decline in the relative weight of imports of intermediate and consumer goods (spare parts, food-stuffs and beverages, durable and semi-durable goods), and an increase in the relative weight of imports of capital goods.

The European countries as a group accounted for 41 percent of Kuwait's imports in 1981, but Japan remained the largest single source of imports, accounting for 22.7

percent of total imports in that year. It was followed by the United States, which accounted for 14 percent of imports. Of the European countries the most important source of imports is the Federal Republic of Germany (12 percent of imports). The United Kingdom, which is a major factor in Gulf trade because of its position as a former imperial power, is nonetheless a minor exporter of goods to Kuwait, accounting for a mere 5.8 percent of Kuwaiti imports. All Arab countries combined provided Kuwait with 3.4 percent of its imports in 1981, the two biggest suppliers being Lebanon and Jordan.

Estimates for 1983 indicate that the level of imports has fallen (for the first time in recent years) by 9.0 percent – a reflection of the deep recession which has resulted in curtailed demand for imported consumer and capital goods. The moderate decline in the market value of the KD in 1984 may keep import demand under control, even if the economy recovers.

10.3 CURRENT ACCOUNT. The balance of merchandise trade deteriorated in 1982 as a result of falling oil exports and (up to that point) continually growing imports. The trade surplus declined to KD 886 million ($3.068 billion).

The services account is believed to have likewise deteriorated in 1982, reflecting lower investment income (as Kuwait's international portfolio shrank slightly and, according to some, became less profitable) and a larger bill for shipping and related sevices.

The other component of the current account is unrequited transfers, both private (mainly foreign workers' remittances to their families abroad) and official (mainly aid to other states). These are reported to have fallen in 1982, as private transfers rose very slightly and official transfers dropped dramatically, resulting in a combined current account surplus officially estimated at KD 1.515 billion ($5.248 billion), less than half the 1981 current account surplus (KD 4.091 billion [$14.537 billion]).

Estimates for 1983 indicate a somewhat larger surplus in the balance of trade (estimated at KD 1.204 billion [$4.115 billion]), and a corresponding deterioration in the balance of services and transfers, resulting in a practically unchanged current account surplus (estimated at KD 1.534 billion [$5.243 billion]).

10.4 CAPITAL ACCOUNT AND OVERALL BALANCE OF PAYMENT POSITION. The nonmonetary capital account (which excludes the government investment account) reversed its usual trend in 1982, with inflows exceeding outflows for the first time in years. This resulted in a capital account surplus estimated officially at KD 454 million ($1.552 billion), as compared to a deficit of KD 112 million ($398.0 million) in 1981.

The government investment account (which includes all foreign assets in the General Reserve Account, and the Reserve for Future Generations) showed a slight surplus (KD 6 million [$20.8 million]) in 1982, compared to a deficit of KD 2.214 billion ($7.867 billion) in 1981.

Balance of Payments Summary
1980 – 83
(KD million)

Current Receipts	**7,177**	**-27.2**	**5,222**	**-2.4**	**5,096**
Exports:	4,446	-29.8	3,121	3.8	3,239
Oil	3,888	-34.6	2,541	8.5	2,757
Other	558	3.9	580	-16.9	482
Investment Income	2,343	-21.8	1,831	-14.2	1,571
Other	388	-30.4	270	5.9	286
Current Payments:	**-3,086**	**20.1**	**-3,707**	**-3.9**	**-3,562**
Imports	-1,878	19.1	-2,236	-9.0	-2,035
Others	-1,208	21.8	-1,471	3.8	-1,527
Current Surplus	**4,091**	**-63.0**	**1,515**	**1.3**	**1,534**
Capital Account	**-2,585**		**224**		**-456**
Government Investment	-2,214		6		150
Other (net)	-371		218		-606
Errors and Omissions	-1,428		-1,174		-1,264
Overall Surplus	**78**		**565**		**-186**

Source: Central Bank of Kuwait

After deducting errors and omissions (which are rather arbitrarily determined) we arrive at a balance of payments surplus officially estimated at KD 565 million ($1.957 billion) for 1982, a considerable improvement over the 1981 figure of KD 78 million ($277.17 million).

Estimates for 1983 indicate a return to capital account deficits. The nonmonetary capital account swung back into deficit (indicating a net export of capital), while the government investment account surplus expanded slightly to KD 150 million ($512.7 million). The capital account thus shows an estimated deficit of KD 456 million ($1.558 billion). After subtracting errors and ommissions, we arrive at an estimating overall balance of payments deficit of KD 186 million ($635.8 million). However, the Central Bank estimates from which these figures are obtained are tentative; while the final figure for the overall balance of payments will probably stand, other current and capital account figures for 1983 will most likely be revised.

10.5 THE KUWAITI DINAR. Kuwait has an independent (unpegged) exchange rate policy, according to which the KD spot exchange rate is fixed daily by the Central Bank (through intervention on the currency market) in accordance with an undisclosed formula. The formula in effect pegs the KD to a basket of major currencies, of which, it has been empirically determined, the most important is by far the US dollar (the currency against which the KD was formerly pegged). Over the period 1973-83, the standard deviation of the KD/dollar exchange rate around its mean in percentage terms was found to be as low as 2.9 percent (compared to 10.9 percent for the Japanese yen, 10.9 percent for the DM, 18.8 percent for the Swiss franc, and 12.6 percent for the pound Sterling).

The market KD/dollar rate ($3.37 to the KD in mid-1984) has fallen in recent months, and some fear it may fall further. This very fear, and persistent rumors of an imminent devaluation of the KD, have encouraged a measure of speculation against the KD. However, though the market rate may continue to deteriorate, an official devaluation does not appear to be probable. Considering Kuwait's current account surplus (over KD 1.5 billion [$5.127 billion] in 1982 and 1983), the Central Bank's foreign assets (KD 6 billion [$20.508 billion] including gold), the adverse effect on the private sector (higher import costs, inflation, higher cost of private transfers abroad, capital losses on KD bonds), and negative psychological impact, most experts regard devaluation as extremely unlikely.

10.6 FOREIGN INVESTMENTS AND FOREIGN AID. As a result of continued current account surpluses, Kuwait has accumulated impressive reserves (currently estimated at $72 billion). While Kuwait's international portfolio has suffered (primarily due to a reduction in liquidity as Kuwait hastened to provide aid to Iraq), Kuwait remains the most sophisticated of the Arab oil producers in investment policy. It has the longest experience in international finance.

The disposition of surplus funds has proceeded through the following channels:

- The London-based Kuwait Investment Office (KIO), established in 1952 (initially called Kuwait Investment Board) by the Ministry of Finance to act as the government's principal overseas investment agent under the direct administration of the Finance Ministry.
- Local commercial banks (active in international markets) and investment companies (primarily the three K's). Some of these are partly or totally government owned.
- Some of the leading international banks and investment firms operating in international markets acting as portfolio managers for Kuwait. These include financial institututions in the U.S., Europe, the Arab World (primarily Bahrain) and the Far East.
- The Kuwait Fund for Arab Economic Development, through which aid has been dispensed to Arab and other countries.

The objectives underlying Kuwait's disposition of foreign funds are:

- Accumulating wealth to ensure the future well-being of Kuwait when its oil revenues dry up.
- Generating a source of income independent of oil that diversifies the sources of government revenue.
- Establishing a major Kuwaiti presence in international (and particularly Eurocredit) markets.
- Expanding the geographic scope of the oil industry through the consolidation of international downstream activities.
- Channeling Kuwait's surplus funds through concessional loans to Arab and friendly Third World countries.

A distinction should be made between bilateral aid (for which provision is made in the state budget) and aid dispensed through KFAED. Bilateral aid goes mainly to Arab "front-line" states, i.e., to the states confronting Israel, and to Iraq; this aid has no bearing on Kuwait's international portfolio. KFAED aid takes the form of concessional loans to Third World states and is included in Kuwait's international portfolio.

Kuwait was the first Arab country to set up a donor agency for dispensing foreign aid; the Kuwait Fund for Arab Economic Development (KFAED) was established in 1961 to dispense soft (concessional) loans to Third World countries. While Arab countries received a major share (57 percent) of aid disbursed by KFAED from January 1962 to June 1982, Asian countries have also been granted loans (24.9 percent of total) by KFAED, as have African countries (17.6 percent of total). KFAED loans finance projects in the areas of agriculture, industry, transportation and infrastructural development. The amount dispensed from January 1962 to June 1982 totalled KD 992 million ($3.4 billion).

The aid dispensed by Kuwait through KFAED is less politically motivated than aid dispensed by Saudi Arabia. Other than an obvious (though not overwhelming) preference for Arab recipients, there is no strong political bias in KFAED aid; Muslim countries are not particularly favored, nor are Communist countries excluded (the People's Republic of China received three loans totalling KD 33.6 million [$117 million] in 1982).

Kuwait was a founding member of the Arab Fund for Economic and Social Development (AFESD), which is headquartered in Kuwait. Kuwait's contribution to AFESD's capital subscriptions totalled $589 million (or 22.6 percent of total) in 1982. Kuwait's contribution to the capital subscriptions of the Banque Arabe pour le Developpement Politique en Afrique totalled $110 million (14.9 percent of total) in 1982, while its contribution to the capital subscriptions of the Islamic Development Bank (IDB) totalled 13.9 percent of total capital in 1982. Kuwait also holds 9.5 percent of the Arab Monetary Fund's shares. Kuwait also dispenses foreign aid through contributions to the Opec Fund for International Economic Development, the International Monetary Fund, and the World Bank.

Estimates of Kuwait's total foreign reserves vary. Official announcements have put these reserves at KD 20.984 billion (approximately $72 billion), of which KD 12.808 billion ($44 billion) was in general reserves, while KD 8.176 billion ($28 billion) was in the Reserves Fund for Future Generations, which cannot be touched for 25 years.

Income on Kuwait's foreign investments was estimated at KD 1.364 billion ($4.7 billion) in 1981-82, lower than 1980-81's KD 1.744 billion ($6.0 billion). The figure for 1982-83 is projected at KD 1.300 billion ($4.4 billion) It appears that the decline (reflecting deteriorating financial conditions worldwide, a reduced liquidity in the portfolio, and some drawing down – now supposedly discontinued – to cover aid to Iraq) may have come to an end. If so, Kuwait can anticipate an income on foreign investment in the neighborhood of $5 billion for the current fiscal year. Investment income is routinely rolled over to the General Reserve Fund.

IV. KUWAIT: STATISTICAL APPENDIX

Table 1.

BASIC INFORMATION

Official name: State of Kuwait

Country Abbreviation: KU

Foreign occupation: British Protectorate 1899-1961

Date of Independence: June 19, 1961

National Flag: Three horizontal green, red, and white stripes with a black trapezium based on the hoist whose shorter base is equal to the width of the white stripe.

National Emblem: A circular badge on which a dhow, a white-sailed craft, appears against a blue sky and white clouds. At the crest appears the name "Dawlat al Kuwait" in Arabic and at the base appears a white falcon.

National Anthem Title: unnamed melody, no words

National Holidays: February 25 National Day
January 1 New Year's Day
Also Muslim New Year's Day and Islamic festivals

Nature of government: Constitutional hereditary emirate with elected National Assembly

Date of Constitution: November 12,1961

Past Leaders: Shaikh Ahmad al-Jabir (1921-1950)
Shaikh Abdullah al-Salim (1950-Nov.24, 1965)
Shaikh Sabah al-Salim Al Sabah (1965-)

Weights & Measures: Metric system

Time: 3 hours ahead of GMT

Currency units: Kuwaiti dinar (KD)= 1,000 fils
$1= KD 0.293 (May 1984)

Languages: Arabic, English

Geographic Facts:
Area: 17,818 sq km (6,880 sq mi)
Bodies of water: none
Capital City: Kuwait City Population: 1,464,000 (1980)

Selected climate parameters:

	Kuwait City
Average Minimum Temp (C)	
Summer (May-Oct)	28.8
Winter (Nov.-April)	7.9
Average Maximum Temp	
Summer	44.8
Winter	18.5

Annual Rainfall (mm): 30mm-220 mm Wettest month: Dec.
Other: Sand and dust storms frequent in summer.

Table 2.

CABINET LIST

Head of State........................Emir Shaikh Jabir al-Ahmad Al Sabah

Crown Prince, Prime Minister...Shaikh Saad al-Abdullah al-Salem Al Sabah
Deputy Premier Foreign
Affairs and Information.........Shaikh Sabah al-Ahmad al-Jabir Al Sabah

Interior.......................Shaikh Nawwaf al-Ahmad al-Jabir Al Sabah
Defense.........................Shaikh Salem al-Sabah al-Salem Al Sabah
Oil...................................Shaikh Ali al-Khalifa Al Sabah

Public Health..............................Abdel-Rahman Abdullah al-Awadi
Social Affairs, Labour & Housing....................Hamad Isa al-Rujaib
Public Works..Abdullah al-Rashid
Electricity & Water..............................Khalaf Ahmad al-Khalaf

Justice, Legal Affairs,
& Administrative Affairs................Shaikh Salman al-Duaij Al Sabah
Finance & Planning..........................Abd al-Latif Yousef al-Hamad
Education.......................................Yacoub Yousef al-Ghunaim
Commerce & Industry....................................Jassem al-Marzouk

Communications..Isa al-Mazidi
Religious Endowments (Awqaf) & Islamic Affairs......Ahmad Saad al-Jasser
Minister of State for Cabinet Affairs.................Abdel-Aziz Husain

DIPLOMATIC REPRESENTATIVES

U.S. Ambassador to Kuwait: Philip J. Griffin (Charges d'Affaires)

Ambasador to U.S.: Shaikh Saud Nasir Al Sabah (1984)

U.N. Ambassador: Mohammed Abdulhassan.

Table 3.

MEMBERSHIP IN REGIONAL AND INTERNATIONAL ORGANIZATIONS

Organization	**Contribution to Capital**
Regional	
Arab Bank for Economic Development in Africa	$110 million (1982)
Arab Fund for Economic and Social Development	169.70 million Kuwaiti Dinars (1982)
Arab Monetary Fund	500 million Arab Accounting Dinars (1983)
Cooperation Council for the Arab States of the Gulf	
Council of Arab Economic Unity	
Islamic Development Bank	252.2 million Islamic Dinars (1982)
Organization of Arab Petroleum Exporting Countries	
Organization of the Islamic Conference	
Organization of Petroleum Exporting Countries	
OPEC Fund for International Development	
International	
United Nations	
International Monetary Fund	
International Bank for Reconstruction and Development	

Table 4.

DEMOGRAPHIC INDICATORS

Population, total (est. mid 1981):	1,464,000
Official census 1980:	1,355,827
Rank in world:	124th
Population, males:	847,962
Population, females:	615,888
Population ages, percent of total	
0-14:	44.4 (1982)
15-59:	53 (1982)
65+:	2.6 (1982)
Urban population:	1,310,000
as percent of total:	88
Rural population:	
as percent of total:	12
Population density (per sq km):	
nationwide	52
rural areas	1,335
Crude birth rates (per 1,000):	39 (1980)
Crude death rates (per 1,000):	5 (1980)
Annual growth rate:	6% (1970-1980)
Infant mortality rate (per 1,000):	2
Total fertility rates (per 1,000):	207.7
Life expectancy, males:	66.14
Life expectancy, females:	71.82
Marriage rate (per 1,000):	5.1
Divorce rate (per 1,000):	1.5

POPULATION OF MAJOR CITIES
(1980)

Major Cities	Population
Ahmadi	232,000
Hawalli	751,000
Jahra	190,000

Sources: MERI. Data taken from World Bank, Demographic Yearbook 1983, UN Monthly Bulletin of statistics.

DEFENSE

Table 5.

KUWAIT MILITARY PERSONNEL AND EQUIPMENT

Commander in Chief:	Emir Shaikh Jabir al-Ahmad Al Sabah
Type of Military Service:	Compulsory 18 months for males between 21 and 30
Chief of Staff:	Major-General Abdullah Farraj al-Ghanim

Army: 10,000

1 armoured brigade
2 mechanized infantry batallions
1 surface-to-surface missile batallion
70 Vickers Mark 1, 10 Centurion, 160 Chieftain main battle tanks
100 Saladin armoured and 80 Ferret scout cars
175 M-113, 130 Saracen armoured personnel carriers
20 AMX Mk F-3 155mm self-propelled howitzers FROG-7 surface-to-surface missile
81mm mortars
HOT, TOW, Vigilant anti-tank guided weapons, SA-7 SAM
(On order: Scorpion light tanks, 188 M-113 armoured personnel carriers 56 M-113 self-propelled TOW vehicles, 4,800 improved TOW anti-tank guided weapons)

Navy: 500 (coastguard) Commander: Habib al-Meel

47 coastal patrol craft (15 armoured)
6 landing craft
(On order: 6 Lurssen TNC-45, 2 FPB-57 attack craft, 6 SRN-6 hovercraft; 12 harbor sport craft, 45 MM-38/-40 Exocet Surface-to-Surface missiles)

Air Force: 1,900

49 combat aircraft
2 FB squadrons with 30 A-4KU
1 interceptor sqadron with 17 Mirage F-1C, 2 F-1B
Transport vehicles: 2 DC-9, 1 L-100-20, 4 L-100-30
3 helicopter sqadrons with 23 SA-342K Gazelle and 9 Puma
Trainers include 9 Strikemaster
1 SAM batallion with Improved HAWK
Air-to-air missiles: R-550 Magic, Sidewinder
Air-to-surface missiles: Super 530, SS-11/-12
(In storage: 12 Lightning, 9 Hunter)
(On order: 12 Mirage F-1C fighters; 6 Super Puma helicopters;
12 AM-39 Exocet air-to-surface missiles)

Para-Military Forces: 18,000 Police

Source: The Military Balance 1983-84

Table 6.

TRADE IN MAJOR CONVENTIONAL WEAPONS
1981-1983

Supplier	Number Ordered	Weapon/Description	Year Ordered	Year Delivered	Number Delivered
France	8	Combattante/FAC	1982	--	--
	12	Mirage F-1C/Fighter	1982	--	--
	32	MM-40 Exocet/ShShM SShM	1980	1982	4
	--	MM-40 Exocet/ShShM SShM	1982	--	--
Germany & France	2	PC-57 Type/PC/FAC	1980	--	--
	6	TNC-45/FAC	1980	--	--
United Kingdom	100	Chieftan-5/MBT	1981	--	--
USA	4,840	BGM-71A TOW/ATM	1982	--	--
	4	L-100-30/Transport	1981	1983	4
	16	M-113-A2/APC	1982	--	--
	2	M-125-A1/APC	1980	--	--

Source: SIPRI Yearbook 1983

Table 7.

KUWAITI MILITARY EXPENDITURE 1973-81 *

	1980 prices (US $mn)	Current Prices (KD mn)	% of GDP
1973	490	74.7*	4.8
1974	858	148	4.5
1975	1,017	191	5.4
1976	1,246	247	6.6
1977	1,361	292	7.3
1978	1,169	276	6.6
1979	1,159	293	4.8
1980	1,265	342	4.7
1981	1,430*	415*	6.0

* Estimates

Source: SIPRI Yearbook 1983.

WATER RESOURCES

Table 8.

TOTAL RAINFALL BY STATIONS
(mm)

	1978	1979	1980	1981	1982	Mean
Kuwait International Airport						
Jan	44.0	51.8	16.8	29.7	31.1	34.7
Feb	3.1	0.5	54.1	29.4	17.1	21.0
Mar	29.3	4.1	16.8	6.3	16.7	14.6
Apr	0.6	0.1	0.6	1.7	2.8	1.1
May	0.6	10.9	0.2	0.4	4.8	3.4
Oct	--	3.2	--	1.8	7.8	2.6
Nov	15.1	--	1.8	9.0	32.8	11.7
Dec	14.1	50.4	41.6	2.1	15.1	24.7
TOTAL	**106.8**	**121.0**	**131.9**	**80.4**	**128.8**	**113.8**
Shuwaikh						
Jan	33.3	44.4	15.8	31.0	29.6	30.8
Feb	3.6	1.7	59.2	29.7	10.3	21.0
Mar	26.2	4.0	6.6	3.7	24.5	13.0
Apr	1.6	--	0.2	3.3	4.5	1.9
May	0.8	8.7	--	0.6	2.0	2.4
Oct	--	29.6	--	3.3	4.3	7.4
Nov	20.3	--	1.3	9.9	15.4	9.4
Dec	18.3	52.5	50.9	4.0	14.3	28.0
TOTAL	**104.1**	**140.9**	**134.0**	**85.5**	**104.9**	**113.9**
Omariyah						
Jan	43.0	52.0	9.8	29.8	30.5	33.0
Feb	4.4	1.4	61.0	32.3	11.5	22.1
Mar	26.5	7.2	5.2	8.8	26.1	14.8
Apr	1.4	0.4	0.6	1.7	7.1	2.2
May	0.9	8.9	--	--	7.0	3.4
Oct	--	11.7	--	2.6	6.0	4.1
Nov	22.1	0.4	1.8	14.6	10.6	9.9
Dec	20.3	48.5	46.3	4.2	14.3	26.7
TOTAL	**118.6**	**131.1**	**124.7**	**94.0**	**113.1**	**116.3**

TOTAL RAINFALL BY STATIONS
(mm)

	1978	1979	1980	1981	1982	Mean
Failaka Island						
Jan	58.3	42.0	9.3	32.6	35.3	35.5
Feb	4.4	0.5	58.8	28.6	19.3	22.3
Mar	14.7	2.2	6.0	6.3	25.1	10.8
Apr	1.0	--	0.7	0.6	5.1	1.5
May	4.0	1.0	--	--	1.5	1.3
Oct	--	55.5	--	12.7	6.8	15.0
Nov	13.7	--	1.3	16.7	82.2	22.8
Dec	13.3	64.7	71.4	3.0	23.5	35.2
TOTAL	**109.4**	**165.9**	**147.5**	**100.5**	**198.8**	**144.4**
Al-Ahmadi						
Jan	53.9	51.6	17.9	25.6	40.2	37.8
Feb	7.5	0.2	34.4	18.8	13.4	14.9
Mar	--	5.9	2.6	5.8	12.0	9.1
Apr	--	0.4	2.1	1.9	4.7	1.8
May	6.1	13.9	--	15.9	--	7.2
Oct	--	2.3	--	--	15.8	3.6
Nov	22.0	0.8	1.1	9.5	14.0	9.6
Dec	20.0	56.3	27.7	4.8	13.8	24.5
TOTAL	**129.0**	**131.4**	**85.8**	**82.3**	**113.9**	**108.5**
Al-Ahmadi Port						
Jan	37.2	53.4	12.0	24.1	23.4	30.0
Feb	5.9	0.2	36.5	13.2	3.1	11.8
Mar	14.7	6.0	5.1	2.8	20.8	9.9
Apr	--	0.2	2.2	2.8	3.4	1.7
May	4.0	6.7	--	4.8	--	3.1
Oct	--	3.0	--	--	12.1	3.0
Nov	16.7	0.1	1.5	11.5	13.6	8.7
Dec	11.3	44.8	21.5	3.1	14.2	19.0
TOTAL	**89.8**	**115.5**	**78.8**	**62.3**	**90.6**	**87.4**

Source: Kuwait Annual Statistical Abstract 1983

Table 9.

PRODUCTION AND CONSUMPTION OF POTABLE & BRACKISH WATER
(million gallons)

	1978	1979	1980	1981	1982
Production					
Potable Water:					
Underground	555	58	126	174	120
Distilled Water	20,198	23,026	23,354	24,936	28,517
Total Production	20,753	23,084	23,480	25,110	28,637
Daily Average	56.8	63.2	64.3	68.8	78.4
Brackish Water:					
Total Production	10,181	10,823	11,319	12,127	14,219
Daily Average	27.9	29.6	31.0	33.2	39.0
Consumption					
Potable:					
Total Consumption	20,699	23,068	23,441	24,917	28,181
Average Daily Consumption	56.8	63.2	64.2	68.3	77.2
Brackish Water:					
Consumption	8,213	9,123	9,750	10,451	12,264
Average Daily Consumption	22.5	25.0	26.7	28.6	33.6

Source: Kuwait Annual Statistical Abstract 1983

ECONOMY

Table 10.

PRINCIPAL ECONOMIC INDICATORS

GDP per capita (1982):	$12,862
Total GDP: (1981 mn $US):	$24,297
GDP average annual growth rate (1960-1970):	5.6%
(1970-1981):	2.3%
Average annual GNP per capita growth rate (1960-81):	-0.4%
Average annual growth rate (1970-81)	
Public consumption:	10.8%
Private consumption:	13.1%
Gross domestic investment:	17.5%
Annual growth rate of inflation (1970-1980):	18.4% (1970-1980)

Source: World Bank Development Report 1983; International Herald Tribune Special Report on Kuwait, April 25, 1983.

Table 11.

COST OF LIVING INDEX
(1972=100)

(Relative Weight)	1975	1976	1977	1978	1979	1980
Foodstuffs (37.1)	153.7	163.7	175.4	182.6	186.4	206.9
Housing & related services (17.7)	106.0	122.8	145.8	164.3	174.7	186.4
Household appliances (2.6)	146.5	149.7	157.2	161.0	164.8	179.8
Durable consumer goods (14.0)	136.8	138.8	150.9	158.7	166.8	169.2
Clothing and cosmetics (14.5)	124.4	135.6	151.8	159.8	178.0	188.4
Transportation & communication (9.6)	120.8	119.2	130.5	141.0	147.0	159.9
Educational, medical, & recreational services (4.5)	118.6	126.0	132.1	144.9	163.5	184.6
General Index (100)	133.7	142.7	156.6	166.4	175.0	188.5

Source: Ministry of Planning, Central Statistical Office

Table 12.

GROSS DOMESTIC PRODUCT AT CURRENT PRICES
(Million KD)

1981

	Total	% Change from 1980	% of Total
Oil Sector	4,125.5	-18.50	61.0
Non-Oil Sector	2,638.8	10.45	39.0
Agriculture & Fisheries	19.0	9.80	0.3
Manufacturing	372.8	-15.25	5.5
Electricity, Gas & Water	27.5	10.00	0.4
Construction	263.0	19.50	3.9
Wholesale & Retail Trade	485.0	3.60	7.2
Restaurants & Hotels	20.4		0.3
Transportation, Storage & Communication	145.5	16.90	2.1
Financial Institutions	216.3	27.95	3.2
Insurance	16.0	10.30	0.2
Other	1,073.3	15.65	15.9
Total GDP	6,763.9	9.20	100.0

1982

	Total	% Change from 1981	% of Total
Oil Sector	2,785.0	-32.5	48.5
Non-Oil Sector	2,951.9	11.9	51.5
Agriculture & Fisheries	21.5	13.2	0.4
Manufacturing	424.2	11.6	7.4
Electricity, Gas & Water	30.1	9.4	0.5
Construction	285.0	8.4	5.0
Wholesale & Retail Trade	521.0	7.4	9.1
Restaurants & Hotels	23.0	12.7	0.4
Transportation, Storage & Communication	181.4	24.6	3.2
Financial Institutions	270.0	24.6	4.7
Insurance	18.0	12.5	0.3
Other	1,177.7	9.7	20.5
Total GDP	5,736.9	-15.2	100.0

Source: Kuwait National Bank Report, 1983.

Table 13.

GROSS DOMESTIC PRODUCT AT CURRENT PRICES
(Million KD)

	1977	1978	1979	1980	1981	1982
Oil Sector	2,483.0	2,520.1	4,433.8	5,156.8	4,110.1	2,785.0
Non-oil sector of which:	1,570.1	1,674.3	2,005.2	2,216.9	2,400.3	2,951.9
Agriculture & Fisheries	13.1	13.5	16.6	17.5	18.6	21.5
Manufacturing	239.5	256.6	366.3	439.6	450.4	424.2
Electricity, gas & water	19.8	22.9	26.2	27.1	29.9	30.1
Construction	158.4	176.1	180.0	185.0	213.0	285.0
Wholesale & retail trade	352.4	318.6	350.5	375.5	470.5	521.0
Transport, storage & communications	77.3	90.0	103.4	119.4	135.7	181.4
Financial institutions	72.8	104.1	135.3	183.5	215.3	270.0
Insurance	11.8	12.0	13.3	15.6	16.5	18.0
Others	624.8	680.5	813.6	853.7	850.4	1,200.8
Total	**4,053.1**	**4,194.4**	**6,439.0**	**7,373.7**	**6,510.4**	**5,736.9**

Source: Kuwait Central Bank 1983

Table 14.

GROSS DOMESTIC PRODUCT BY INDUSTRIAL ORIGIN AT CONSTANT 1972 PRICES
(Million KD)

	1977	1978	1979	1980	1981
Agriculture	5.5	6.4	7.7	7.8	--
Mining	549.0	593.9	695.0	462.8	--
Manufacturing	98.9	107.8	127.6	136.5	--
Construction	103.7	105.8	102.9	100.8	--
Electricity, Gas, Water	20.8	24.6	28.6	30.0	--
Transport & Communications	83.2	91.1	96.5	102.3	--
Trade & Finance	282.9	258.4	274.2	291.1	--
Public Administration & Defense	383.9	397.7	415.0	475.7	--

Source: World Bank Economic Data 1983.

BANKING AND FINANCE

Table 15.

FINANCIAL SURVEY
(Million KD)

INTERNATIONAL LIQUIDITY

	1977	1978	1979	1980	1981
Foreign exchange reserves	2,005.9	1,733.8	2,356.7	3,404.9	3,549.4
Gold (mn fine troy ounces)	2.511	2.525	2.539	2.539	2.539
Gold (national valuation)	112.1	116.3	116.1	116.8	112.6
Reserve position in Fund	877.2	766.6	513.4	523.5	476.9
SDR's	---	---	---	---	41.2
MONETARY SURVEY					
Foreign Assets (Net)	1,224.5	1,322.7	1,417.9	1,837.8	2,145.8
Claims on Private Sector	1,236.7	1,564.1	2,123.6	2,676.5	3,459.0
Money	490.7	636.4	669.4	720.8	1,290.2
Quasi-Money	1,078.2	1,314.0	1,593.3	2,136.8	2,575.8
Government Deposits	440.0	374.0	586.0	833.6	835.2
Other Items (Net)	452.5	562.3	692.9	823.1	903.7
COMMERCIAL BANKS					
Claims on Private Sector	1,236.7	1,564.1	2,123.6	2,676.5	3,459.0
Foreign Assets	822.4	1,214.4	1,407.7	1,880.1	2,245.5
Reserves	271.0	122.7	143.3	221.7	321.6
Foreign Liabilities	419.8	601.5	803.9	1,134.3	1,262.3
Demand Deposits	339.8	459.4	453.5	469.5	1,005.5
Time and Saving Deposits	1,078.0	1,314.0	1,593.3	2,136.8	2,575.8
Government Deposits	114.9	99.2	139.9	164.9	163.9
Capital Accounts	197.4	218.4	268.6	337.0	411.0
Other Items (Net)	180.2	208.6	415.4	535.8	607.6
CENTRAL BANK					
Foreign Assets	821.9	709.8	814.1	1,091.9	1,162.6
Reserves	431.5	318.7	379.2	506.2	679.3
Capital accounts	8.0	27.9	27.9	30.0	44.3
Government deposits	325.1	274.8	446.1	668.7	671.3
Other Items (Net)	57.3	88.4	-39.0	-113.0	-232.2

Source: International Financial Statistics July 1984

FINANCIAL SURVEY
(Million KD)

INTERNATIONAL LIQUIDITY

	1982	1983	Apr/84
Foreign exchange reserves	5,335.9	4,425.49	4,297.5
Gold (mn fine troy ounces)	2.539	2.539	2.539
Gold (national valuation)	109.8	108.4	--
Reserve position in Fund	476.9	508.6	762.9
SDR's	68.8	37.3	43.7

MONETARY SURVEY

	1982	1983	Apr/84
Foreign Assets (Net)	2,444.7	2,288.0	2,313.8
Claims on Private Sector	4,277.7	4,743.1	4,745.8
Money	1,247.6	1,179.6	1,145.5
Quasi-Money	2,935.1	3,188.2	3,249.0
Government Deposits	1,189.9	1,115.6	1,184.8
Other Items (Net)	1,349.7	1,547.7	1,480.1

COMMERCIAL BANKS

	1982	1983	Apr/84
Claims on Private Sector	4,277.7	4,743.1	4,745.8
Foreign Assets	2,251.1	2,301.2	2,104.0
Reserves	625.9	372.5	255.3
Foreign Liabilities	1,526.5	1,550.4	1,248.0
Demand Deposits	904.9	839.0	800.1
Time and Saving Deposits	2,935.1	3,188.2	3,249.0
Government Deposits	393.8	362.4	366.2
Capital Accounts	576.9	664.4	690.9
Other Items (Net)	817.5	812.5	750.9

CENTRAL BANK

	1982	1983	Apr/84
Foreign Assets	1,720.1	1,537.2	1,457.8
Reserves	1,097.7	841.0	701.7
Capital accounts	53.2	149.3	251.3
Government deposits	796.1	753.2	818.6
Other Items (Net)	-226.9	-206.4	750.9

Table 16.

ALLOCATION OF BANKING CREDIT AMONG MAIN ECONOMIC SECTORS
(Million KD)

Sector	1978	1979	1980	1981	1982
Trade	1,441.2	1,889.4	2,339.2	3,105.3	3,820.1
Industry	216.5	314.2	499.3	641.8	889.1
Construction	907.6	1,214.5	1,474.9	2,261.8	2,593.5
Agriculture & Fishing	75.6	113.9	145.6	156.1	183.7
Financial Services and Others	1,037.9	1,567.8	2,132.7	2,558.9	3,794.4
Personal	1,003.9	1,701.2	2,188.1	2,966.2	4,180.1
Total Credit	**4,683.6**	**6,901.0**	**8,779.8**	**11,290.1**	**15,460.9**
As Percent of Total Credit:					
Trade	31.0	27.4	26.6	27.6	24.7
Industry	4.6	4.6	5.7	5.7	5.6
Construction	19.5	17.6	16.8	16.5	16.8
Agriculture & Fishing	1.6	1.7	1.7	1.4	1.1
Personal	21.2	26.1	25.0	26.1	27.0

Source: Kuwait Annual Statistical Abstract 1983

Table 17.

ESTIMATES OF INVESTMENT AND SAVINGS 1975-79
(Million KD)

	1975	1976	1977	1978	1979
Public investment	200.0	288.9	460.5	539.8	507.9
Private investment	217.6	274.1	393.5	245.2	183.1
Change in stocks	26.1	72.1	128.9	-7.5	6.2
Gross domestic investment	443.7	635.1	982.9	777.5	697.2
Net exports of goods and services	1,899.0	1,742.4	1,158.0	1,308.0	3,365.0
Net factor income received from abroad	224.0	441.0	518.0	734.0	920.0
Total savings	**2566.7**	**2818.5**	**2658.5**	**2819.5**	**4982.2**
Total savings as per cent of GNP	69.2	65.8	58.2	57.2	67.7

Source: Ministry of Planning

Table 18.

EXCHANGE RATES
(Market Rate/Par or Central Rate; $US per Dinar)

1976	3.4849
1977	3.5703
1978	3.6792
1979	3.6615
1980	3.6860
1981	3.5535
1982	3.4638
1983	3.2648
1984	
Jan	3.3977
Feb	3.4233
Mar	3.4182
Apr	3.4146

Source: International Financial Statistics June 1984

Table 19.

INTEREST RATE SURVEY
(in percent per annum)

	1 day	1 week	1 month	3 months	12 months
March of:					
1979	5.42	6.65	6.54	7.46	7.73
1980	6.41	10.48	12.43	12.93	12.75
1981	5.35	8.58	10.61	11.06	11.22
1982	5.05	7.42	9.10	10.46	11.12
1983	5.17	5.72	5.85	6.10	7.24
1984	5.84	7.10	7.21	7.25	7.32

Source: Central Bank of Kuwait

Table 20.

KUWAIT PRIVATE SECTOR DEPOSITS
(Figures at year end)

Item	1981	1982	1983	%Change 1982-83
Total in KD	2,987.8	3,507.1	3,429.7	-2.2
Demand	930.1	837.0	772.9	-7.7
Savings	307.7	336.8	406.1	20.6
Time	1,725.2	2,298.5	2,217.9	-3.5
CD's	24.9	34.7	32.8	-5.5
Deposits if Foreign Currencies	595.2	333.0	597.5	79.5
TOTAL DEPOSITS	3,583.0	3,840.1	4,027.2	4.9

Source: Central Bank of Kuwait Economic Report 1983

BUDGET AND PLANNING

Table 21.

FIVE YEAR DEVELOPMENT PLAN 1976/77 – 1980/81
(Billion KD at 1975-76 prices)

	Amount	Per Cent
Total investment allocations for fixed capital formation	4.441	100
Public sector	3.393	76.4
Private sector	1.048	23.6
Allocations for the rise in stocks	0.444	--
Distribution of total investment by economic sector		
Oil and gas sector	0.765	17.2
Manufacturing other than oil	0.910	20.5
Transportation and communication	0.782	17.6
Water and electricity	0.537	12.1
Construction	1.377	31.0
Other	0.070	1.6

Source: Ministry of Planning and Central Bank of Kuwait

Table 22.

REVENUE AND EXPENDITURE IN STATE BUDGET
(Million KD)

	1981/82	1982/83	1983/84	1984/85
Revenues				
Oil & Gas	5,096.7	2,967.0	2,787.6	2,912
Other	182.3	239.0	249.4	315
Total	**5,279.0**	**3,206.0**	**3,037.0**	**3,227**
Expenditure				
State Expenditure	3,007.7	3,113.5	3,376.3	3,654
Reserve Fund for Future Generations	1,500.0	320.6	303.7	323
State General Reserve	696.3	--	--	--
Kuwait Fund for Arab Economic Development	75.0	30.0	30.0	30
Total	**5,279.0**	**3,464.1**	**3,710.0**	**4,007**

Source: Kuwait Ministry of Planning

Table 23.

BUDGET ALLOCATION BY SECTOR
(Thousand KD)

	1981/82	1982/83	1983/84
Head of State	8,000	8,000	8,000
Amiri Diwan	4,896	5,415	6,019
Office of the Comptroller	1,227	1,338	1,535
Council of Ministers	3,807	5,399	6,105
National Council for Culture Arts, & Literature	2,103	2,075	2,239
Fatwa & Legislation Dept.	1,230	1,336	1,415
Ministry of Planning	21,833	27,904	40,335
Employees' Bureau	12,205	15,157	23,234
Ministry of Foreign Affairs	23,917	20,170	23,948
Ministry of Finance			
general administration	341,965	193,878	196,331
general accounts	785,851	818,495	781,167
customs department	11,400	11,030	13,156
Ministry of Oil	3,285	90,505	51,842
Ministry of Commerce & Industry	44,500	44,326	46,438
Ministry of Defense	192,490	214,150	258,469
National Guard	10,939	11,388	14,058
Ministry of the Interior	99,935	101,875	126,770
Ministry of Justice	9,500	10,635	10,700
Ministry of Endowments & Islamic Affairs	9,520	9,631	11,332
Ministry of Education	221,500	246,050	266,057
Ministry of Information	40,050	39,247	43,640
Ministry of Public Health	171,756	191,500	202,508
Ministry of Social Affairs	43,200	48,870	48,818
Ministry of Housing	1,579	1,261	1,290
Ministry of Electricity & Water	341,570	375,930	833,152
electric power stations & desalination plants	197,100	243,070	
Ministry of Comunications			
telegraphs & telephones	59,294	57,589	80,141
posts	6,280	6,387	7,794
civil aviation	10,135	9,846	9,826
Ministry of Public Works	260,250	231,512	259,303
Total	**2,941,317**	**3,043,860**	**3,297,922**

Source: Ministry of Finance

Table 24.

DEVELOPMENT EXPENDITURE BY SECTORS *

(Million KD)

Sector	1979/80		1980/81		1981/82		1982/83		1983/84	
	C	%	C	%	C	%	B	%	B	%
Administrative Services	12.3	2.7	24.5	5.0	18.7	3.0	20.5	2.8	27.6	3.3
Financial and Commercial Services	3.3	0.7	3.0	0.6	2.9	0.5	4.6	0.6	2.8	0.4
Defence, Security and Justice	3.9	0.9	2.8	0.6	2.7	0.4	3.1	0.4	8.4	1.0
Educational and Cultural Services	15.0	3.2	17.9	3.6	11.1	1.8	21.1	2.9	32.7	3.9
Health Services	10.7	2.3	8.5	1.7	8.1	1.3	18.0	2.5	19.1	2.3
Social and Religious Services	12.5	2.7	10.7	2.2	20.4	3.2	16.7	2.3	20.0	2.4
Housing and Related Facilities /1	136.5	29.4	103.0	20.9	123.5	19.6	235.9	32.3	195.5	23.4
Electricity and Water	147.5	31.8	179.7	36.5	293.0	46.6	338.2	46.3	377.0	45.1
Transport and Communications	97.0	20.9	102.1	20.7	108.0	17.2	36.0	4.9	122.9	14.7
Industry	22.9	4.9	23.4	4.7	20.8	3.3	30.4	4.2	27.1	3.2
Agriculture and Fishing	2.4	0.5	17.2	3.5	19.3	3.1	1.3	0.2	1.8	0.2
Other Unclassified	--	--	--	--	--	--	4.4	0.6	0.5	0.1
Total	**464.0**	**100**	**492.8**	**100**	**628.5**	**100**	**730.2**	**100**	**835.4**	**100**

* Includes construction expenditure by ministries and related departments in institutions and authorities with attached or independent budgets.
/1 Includes the Public Housing Authority
B Budget Value
C Closing Account Value

Source: Ministry of Finance

Table 25.

CURRENT EXPENDITURE BY SECTOR
(Million KD)

Sector	**1979/80**		**1980/81**		**1981/82**		**1982/83**		**1983/84**	
	C	**%**	**C**	**%**	**C**	**%**	**B**	**%**	**B**	**%**
Finance	228	17.2	127	8.6	138	6.3	165	6.3	193	6.8
Defense	334	25.2	336	22.7	425	19.4	467	17.8	408	14.4
Education	188	14.2	212	14.3	246	11.3	287	10.9	324	11.4
Health	101	7.6	117	7.9	152	6.9	182	6.9	189	6.7
Social	116	8.7	217	18.3	271	12.4	307	11.7	339	11.9
Housing	46	3.5	49	3.3	57	2.6	67	2.6	94	3.3
Economic	313	23.8	368	24.9	902	41.1	1,150	43.8	1,293	45.5
Total	**1,326**		**1,480**		**2,190**		**2,624**		**2,839**	**100**

C Closing Account Value
B Budget Value
Figures are rounded; table excludes expenditure for land acquisition and foreign transfers.

Source: Central Bank of Kuwait

ECONOMIC ASSISTANCE

Table 26.

DEVELOPMENT ASSISTANCE FROM KUWAIT

Year	Millions of U.S. dollars	% of GNP
1975	976	8.11
1976	621	4.56
1977	1,517	10.02
1978	1,270	7.37
1979	1,055	4.09
1980*	1,188	3.88

*Provisional

Source: World Development Report 1982

Table 27.

SECTORAL AND GEOGRAPHICAL DISTRIBUTION OF LOANS GIVEN BY THE KUWAIT FUND FOR ARAB ECONOMIC DEVELOPMENT
(Million KD)

Jan 1962 - June 1982

	Arab Countries	African Countries	Asian Countries	Other Countries
Agriculture	127.78	38.01	23.00	3.70
Transport	184.35	84.83	44.95	2.13
Electricity	91.40	29.87	147.05	--
Industry	123.49	17.50	19.91	--
Water & Sewage	27.30	4.00	12.25	--
Total	**565.19**	**174.21**	**247.16**	**5.83**
Percent	57.0	17.6	24.9	0.5

Source: Kuwait Annual Statistical Abstract 1983

Table 28.

KUWAIT FUND FOR ARAB ECONOMIC DEVELOPMENT LOANS COMMITTED, 1982/83
(Million KD)

		Purpose:
Arab Countries:		
Dijoubti	4.5	Boulaos power station
Jordan	10.0	Fifth power project
Tunisia	2.8	Eisckel Lake plains drainage
Tunisia	7.5	Siliana dam
African Countries:		
Botswana	2.9	Morupule power project
Burundi	1.0	Rural development
Guinea Bissau	1.25	Bissalanca airport
Kenya	8.0	Bura irrigation & settlement
Niger	4.5	Birni N'Konni irrigation
Rwanda	5.5	Butare-Cyangugu highway
Senegal	6.0	Phosphate fertilizer plant
Senegal	3.0	Rural water wells
Togo	5.0	Natchamba-Kara-Ketao-Pagouda highway
Upper Volta	4.0	Fada-N'Gourma-Niger border road
Zimbabwe	3.3	Hoyuya, Nyadiri and Copper Queen North Settlement
Asian Countries:		
Bangladesh	10.0	Ashunganj power project
Bhutan	2.7	Gedu wood mfg. project
China	10.0	Hunan wood-based panel plant
China	14.3	Ninggou cement works
China	13.3	Urunqi fertiliser plant
China	6.0	Xiamen airport
India	14.3	Thal fertilizer plant
Pakistan	4.0	Irrigation, Baluchistan
Sri Lanka	12.9	Mahaweli River development
Thailand	5.5	Chiew Larn Hydroelectric plant
Turkey	6.0	Izmir water supply
Turkey	5.5	Trans-Turkey highway
Cyprus	2.4	Limassol bypass, rural roads
Total	**176.1**	

Source: KFAED

ENERGY SECTOR

Table 29.

ENERGY OUTLOOK

Crude Oil Reserves (1984):	63.9 billion bbls
Natural Gas Reserves (1984):	877.92 bn cu m
Production (1981):	89.0 mn tce
Consumption (1981):	6.7 mn tce
Net exports (1981):	75.5 mn tce
Finite Reserves:	13,941.1 mn tce
OPEC Quota (1983):	1,050 '000 b/d
Installed production capacity	2,900 '000 b/d
Maximum sustainable production capacity:	2,500 '000 b/d
Available productive capacity: (includes share of Neutral Zone)	1,250 '000 b/d
Number of producing wells (1983):	530
Number of refineries (1984):	5
Crude refining capacity	622.8 '000 b/cd
Catalytic reforming capacity	48.1 '000 b/cd

Source: MERI. Data taken from API, Petroleum Encyclopedia 1983, Oil and Gas Journal, International Energy Statistical Review 6/1984.

Average annual growth rate of energy production (1974-79):	-0.2%
Average annual growth rate of energy consumption (1974-1979):	9.3%

Source: Kuwait Central Bank; OAPEC

Table 30.

ENERGY SUPPLY AND DEMAND

	Unit	1978	1979	1980	1981	1982
Production						
crude oil	'000 b/d	2,128	2,496	1,595	1,125	822
oil products /1	00 b/d	411	539	435	342	459
natural gas	mn cu m/d	99.96	117.15	78.69	56.95	41.43
Consumption						
oil products	'000 b/d	37	41	45	---	
natural gas	mn cu m/d	61.78	85.10	66.14	49.98	37.16
Exports						
crude oil	'000 b/d	1,761	2,083	1,303	814	369
oil products /2	'000 b/d	327	424	343	255	354
LPG	'000 b/d	38	127	102	52	32

/1 Includes LPG production
/2 Excludes LPG exports

Source: Kuwait Central Bank

Table 31.

ELECTRICAL ENERGY PRODUCED AND CONSUMED

	1978	1979	1980	1981	1982
Installed Capacity (MW)	2,128	2,578	2,578	2,686	2,686
Maximum Load (MW)	1,595	1,950	2,100	2,290	2,590
Total Energy Generated (million KW/H)	6,990	8,616	9,023	10,015	11,699
Consumption by Power Stations (million KW/H)	840	1,079	1,058	1,180	1,344
Domestic Consumption (million KW/H)	6,150	7,537	7,965	8,835	10,355
Utilization Coefficient (percent)	75.0	75.6	81.5	85.3	96.4
Load Factor (percent)	50.0	50.4	48.9	49.9	51.6

$$\text{Utilization Coefficient} = \frac{\text{Maximum Load}}{\text{Installed Capacity}} \times 100$$

$$\text{Load Factor} = \frac{\text{Generated Energy}}{8{,}760 \times \text{Maximum Load}} \times 100$$

(8,784 hours in a leap year)

Source: Kuwait Annual Statistical Abstract 1983

Table 32.

PETROLEUM PRODUCTION BY COMPANY
(million bbl)

Petroleum Company	1978	1979	1980	1981	1982	1983*
Kuwait Oil Company	691.1	807.8	508.4	343.4	242.8	135.7
Kuwait Oil Company (Wafra)	29.5	30.5	28.7	27.7	24.1	12.4
Arabian Oil Co.	56.3	72.7	70.0	40.1	33.1	19.6
Total	776.9	911.0	607.1	411.2	300.2	165.6

Source: Ministry of Oil
*Figures represent Jan.-June production

Table 33.

PRODUCTION AND EXPORTS OF LIQUIFIED GASES BY TYPE
(thousand bbl)

	1978	1979	1980	1981	1982
Production:					
Natural Gasoline	5,415	9,875	7,462	5,463	3,914
Propane	7,238	21,879	17,381	9,564	4,938
Butane	6,616	14,579	10,904	6,976	5,060
Liquified Pentane	--	42	16	--	372
Total	**19,269**	**46,375**	**35,763**	**22,003**	**14,284**
Exports:					
Natural Gasoline	--	6,626	7,462	--	--
Propane	7,328	18,760	17,381	11,122	6,013
Butane	6,244	13,364	10,904	7,665	5,585
Liquified Pentane	--	--	16	--	--
Total	**13,572**	**38,750**	**35,763**	**18,787**	**11,598**

Source: Kuwait Annual Statistical Abstract 1983

Table 34.

PRODUCTION REFINED PETROLEUM PRODUCTS BY TYPE
(thousand bbl)

Product	1978	1979	1980	1981	1982
Naptha	18,581	23,033	17,045	13,116	23,137
Benzine	7,458	8,834	7,947	8,255	10,196
Kerosene	10,608	11,979	11,110	7,451	7,694
Aviation Kerosene	3,104	6,931	4,175	5,788	6,346
Gas Oil	27,217	26,178	25,522	23,822	40,044
Diesel Oil	2,943	4,689	1,964	1,306	1,757
Fuel Oil	58,334	66,095	53,109	40,443	61,443
Asphalt	729	963	1,181	1,526	1,237
Others	1,551	1,918	1,075	749	2,600
Total	**130,525**	**150,620**	**123,128**	**102,456**	**153,424**
Sulphur (ton)	100	114	82,230	108,989	140,644

Source: Kuwait Annual Statistical Abstract 1983

Table 35.

EXPORTS OF CRUDE OIL ACCORDING TO IMPORTING COUNTRIES
(thousand bbl)

Importing Country	**1978**	**1978**	**1980**	**1981**	**1982**
Kuwait Share	5,114	4,793	3,613	2,418	--
Arab Countries	3,072	12,600	3,006	7,560	3,198
U.K.	72,003	57,486	45,428	16,323	--
France	20,227	32,340	22,843	7,119	--
Holland	68,211	94,752	59,821	27,627	9,242
Italy	65,135	73,829	1,771	2,522	8,877
Ireland	25,927	24,294	4,132	1,006	--
W. Germany	4,920	3,979	3,455	3,006	--
Spain	8,800	6,748	7,449	2,203	--
Romania	--	--	4,097	4,938	--
Others	8,339	4,033	366	3,072	--
Total European Countries	**273,562**	**297,461**	**149,584**	**67,816**	**22,729**
U.S.A.	5,490	5,393	7,469	--	--
Canada	--	6,023	5,888	2,330	--
Brazil	25,511	18,135	25,743	9,049	6,766
Uruguay	2,662	1,817	--	--	--
Others	1,409	--	--	--	--
Total American Countries	**35,072**	**31,368**	**39,091**	**11,379**	**6,766**
Japan	176,717	208,507	84,180	89,886	30,295
Singapore	9,307	42,529	44,485	19,178	1,102
South Korea	54,902	58,616	49,723	36,378	18,515
Taiwan	49,685	55,425	55,635	50,260	37,216
Philippines	12,334	10,004	8,366	6,779	6,837
Thailand	5,132	4,432	1,103	--	--
Malaysia	7,464	16,628	3,157	--	--
Others	--	--	818	1,106	--
Total Asian Countries	**315,541**	**396,141**	**247,737**	**203,587**	**93,965**
African Countries	**753**	**5,195**	**3,007**	**480**	**389**
Australia	8,294	9,687	3,944	3,211	106
New Zealand	1,425	2,003	2,186	596	--
Total Oceanic Countries	**9,719**	**11,690**	**6,130**	**3,807**	**106**
Other Countries	--	1,067	9,293	--	7,448
Grand Total	**642,833**	**760,315**	**461,461**	**297,047**	**134,601**

Source: Kuwait Annual Statistical Abstract 1983

Table 36.

EXPORTS OF OIL REFINERY PRODUCTS: 1978-1982
(Thousand bbl)

IMPORTING COUNTRIES	1978	1979	1980	1981	1982
U.K.	781	1,191	1,969	2,857	3,233
Holland	7,154	5,992	5,276	3,271	8,638
Italy	12,330	16,289	6,680	6,236	18,587
W. Germany	2,964	3,326	3,295	1,577	2,282
Denmark	2,493	--	--	--	--
France	--	570	1,380	754	5,292
Others	439	--	848	622	647
Total European Countries	**26,161**	**27,368**	**19,348**	**15,317**	**37,679**
Japan	24,490	24,790	26,753	9,588	12,201
Indonesia	2,080	7,831	7,020	5,553	--
Singapore	1,276	66	1,283	2,242	11,664
South Korea	1,634	2,545	2,704	1,660	1,240
Taiwan	5,961	6,235	5,198	3,838	769
Philippines	615	6,480	6,655	5,335	2,152
Thailand	575	--	--	--	390
Hong Kong	475	1,536	--	--	--
India	6,526	3,719	5,607	6,861	6,679
Pakistan	9,237	11,081	10,726	9,955	13,489
Others	5,316	1,422	1,652	109	644
Total Asian Countries	**58,185**	**65,705**	**67,598**	**45,141**	**49,228**
U.S.A.	--	--	219	--	--
Brazil	644	933	588	308	2,836
Argentina	--	--	155	--	--
Others	--	--	--	--	--
Total American Countries	**810**	**933**	**962**	**308**	**2,836**
Australia	5,798	6,599	9,091	7,649	9,778
New Zealand	980	813	1,297	658	584
Total Oceanic Countries	**6,778**	**7,412**	**10,388**	**8,307**	**10,362**
Tanzania	253	--	186	--	360
Others	1,806	904	--	--	108
Total African Countries	**2,059**	**904**	**186**	**--**	**468**
Kuwait	--	529	19	864	--
Iraq	1,201	1,231	158	--	--
South Yemen	1,756	1,678	3,258	836	--
Muscat and Oman	60	--	--	--	--
United Arab Emirates	2,955	4,704	3,037	3,085	8,456
Others	2,185	2,708	1,931	1,444	1,264
Total Arab Countries	**8,157**	**10,850**	**8,403**	**6,229**	**9,720**
Other Countries	3,753	3,051	3,121	8,551	13,293
Total	**105,903**	**116,223**	**110,006**	**83,853**	**123,586**
Bankers	15,357	18,450	13,047	9,349	5,549
Grand Total	**121,260**	**134,673**	**123,053**	**93,202**	**129,135**

Source: Kuwait Annual Statistical Abstract 1983

Table 37.

LOCAL CONSUMPTION OF PETROLEUM PRODUCTS
(bbl)

Products	1978	1979	1980	1981	1982
Liquified Gas	--	2,275,156	2,464,000	--	--
Gasoline Premium	3,619,067	6,758,811	7,715,000	6,475,446	6,074,024
Kerosene	896,777	3,246,275	2,921,000	686,160	955,080
Gas Oil	1,883,470	3,004,556	4,005,000	6,110,986	8,652,746
Fuel Oil	--	569	--	--	--
Diesel Oil	--	--	--	--	--
Asphalt	--	925,924	1,223,000	--	--
Others	209,434	93,000	--	--	--
Total	**6,608,748**	**16,211,384**	**18,328,000**	**13,272,592**	**15,681,850**

Source: Kuwait Annual Statistical Abstract 1983

Table 38.

CRUDE OIL PRODUCTION: UPDATE
(thousand bbl)

1975	760,700	June	31,200
1976	785,000	July	33,600
1977	718,100	Aug	36,600
1978	776,900	Sept	37,500
1979	911,000	Oct	40,500
1980	607,200	Nov	38,000
1981	411,200	Dec	38,000
1982	72,600	1984	
1983	224,100	Jan	35,030
		Feb	35,815
		Mar	39,990
		Apr	36,000
		May	34,100

Source: Petroleum Economist August 1984

Table 39.

SUMMARY OF PETROLEUM MOVEMENT
Year End Totals
(thousand bbl)

ITEM	**1978**	**1979**	**1980**	**1981**	**1982**
Crude Petroleum:					
Production	777,090	911,208	607,268	411,174	300,221
Refinery Supplies	133,385	151,057	124,614	104,967	154,330
Exported	642,883	760,315	461,461	297,047	134,601
Refined Products:					
Production	130,525	150,621	123,128	102,456	153,424
Exported	105,903	116,223	110,006	83,853	123,586
Bunkers	15,357	18,450	13,047	9,349	5,549
Local Consumption	13,451	16,211	18,328	13,272	15,682
LNG Products	19,268	46,374	35,763	22,003	14,284
LNG Exports	13,572	38,749	N.A.	18,787	11,598
Natural Gas (mn cu m):					
Production	11,124.8	13,037.8	8,781.1	6,330.2	4,608.5
Local Consumption	6,832.1	9,469.4	7,364.3	5,560.7	4,130.6
Flared Gas	4,292.7	3,568.5	1,416.8	769.5	477.9

Daily Average

ITEM	**1978**	**1979**	**1980**	**1981**	**1982**
Crude Petroleum:					
Production	2,129,013	2,496,460	1,663,747	1,126,504	822,523
Refinery Supplies	365,438	413,854	341,408	287,580	422,821
Exported	1,761,186	2,038,027	1,264,276	813,827	368,769
Refined Products:					
Production	357,602	412,660	337,336	280,701	420,339
Exported	290,145	318,419	301,386	229,734	338,592
Bunkers	42,074	50,548	35,745	25,613	15,203
Local Consumption	38,852	44,414	50,213	36,361	42,964
LNG Products	52,789	127,053	97,980	60,282	39,134
LNG Exports	37,183	106,163	N.A.	51,471	31,775
Natural Gas (mn cu m):					
Production	30.47	35.71	24.04	17.33	12.63
Local Consumption	18.69	25.94	20.16	15.24	11.29

Source: Kuwait Annual Statistical Abstract 1983

Table 40.

OFFICIAL CRUDE OIL SALES: PRICES AND CREDIT TERMS 1974-82

	KOC	Arabian Oil Company	
	Kuwait Export 31°	Khafji 28°	Hout 35°
1974	10.36	10.29	10.51
1975	11.30	11.15	11.50
1976			
Jan 1	11.30	11.15	11.50
June 1	11.23	11.05	11.50
1977			
Jan 1	12.37	12.03	12.69
July	12.37	12.10	12.69
1978			
Jan 1	12.27	12.03	12.69
Oct 1	12.22	12.03	12.69
1979			
Jan 1	12.83	12.53	13.33
Oct 1	21.43	21.13	21.93
1980			
Jan 1	27.50	27.20	28.00
July 1	31.50	31.20	32.00
1981			
Jan 1	35.50	35.20	36.00
Nov 1	33.00	31.65	34.01
1982			
Jan 1	32.30	31.03	34.01

Source: Central Bank of Kuwait

INDUSTRY

Table 41.

PRODUCTION AND SALES OF SELECTED MANUFACTURING INDUSTRIES
FOOD MANUFACTURING AND SALES
(thousand tons)

	1978	1979	1980	1981	1982
Flour:					
Production	122.6	153.7	155.6	200.4	210.1
Local Sales	121.9	131.4	136.2	137.9	144.2
Exports	3.0	21.4	18.8	61.8	67.6
Bran:					
Production	23.0	28.9	31.8	35.9	39.6
Local Sales	23.5	32.0	33.9	35.9	39.7
Exports	--	--	--	--	--
Macaroni:					
Production	1.9	1.9	1.7	2.6	2.9
Local Sales	1.6	1.5	2.2	1.6	1.9
Exports	0.1	0.1	0.7	0.8	1.1
Biscuits:					
Production	1.9	1.9	1.7	2.6	2.9
Local Sales	2.1	2.4	2.5	3.1	2.3
Exports	0.2	0.2	0.3	0.5	0.6
Bread:					
Production	N.A.	6.3	6.8	6.9	6.7
Local Sales	6.1	6.3	6.8	6.9	6.7
Exports	--	--	--	--	--
Table Salt:					
Production	18.9	19.7	20.5	18.6	19.3
Local Sales	--	--	--	--	--
Exports	--	--	--	--	--

Source: Kuwait Annual Statistical Abstract 1983

Table 42.

MANUFACTURE AND SALES OF INDUSTRIAL CHEMICALS

	1978	1979	1980	1981	1982
Chlorine (1,000 tons):					
Production	7.0	8.2	8.0	7.9	7.7
Caustic Soda (1,000 tons):					
Production	8.0	9.2	9.1	8.9	8.7
Hydrogen Gas (mn cu m):					
Production	2.3	2.6	2.6	2.5	2.4
Hypochlorite Sodium (mn gals):					
Production	2.61	2.46	3.00	2.15	1.18
Hydorchloric Acid (mn gals):					
Production	0.34	0.29	0.24	0.42	0.39
Ammonium Hydroxide (1,000 metric tons):					
Production	522.9	502.0	331.1	463.7	414.3
Exports	124.8	107.2	71.0	147.7	142.2
Sulphuric Acid (1,000 metric tons):					
Production	N.A.	N.A.	N.A.	4.8	8.9
Local Sales	6.6	7.2	6.7	3.4	4.5
Exports	N.A.	N.A.	N.A.	6.0	4.4
Detergents (1,000 metric tons):					
Production	1.00	1.09	1.64	1.90	1.65
Local Sales	1.04	1.08	1.59	1.89	1.72
Standard Accumulators (1,000 units):					
Production	24.7	31.0	32.7	28.5	25.7
Local Sales	23.3	31.0	30.4	27.6	26.1
Exports	1.6	2.0	2.5	0.09	--
Ammonium Sulphate--Fertilizer (1,000 metric tons):					
Production	--	12.0	--	--	--
Exports	3.5	12.5	2.1	--	--
Urea--Fertilizer (1,000 metric tons):					
Production	663.7	662.1	466.2	463.8	436.3
Exports	674.3	626.1	396.1	382.8	426.4

Source: Kuwait Annual Statistical Abstract 1983

Table 43.

MANUFACTURE OF CEMENT, LIME, AND PLASTER

	1978	1979	1980	1981	1982
Cement (1,000 tons)	621.3	1,040.2	1,307.7	1,549.4	1,552.9
Hydrated Lime (1,000 tons)	3.8	5.6	17.7	21.6	10.2
Sand Lime Bricks (1,000 cu m)	262.5	357.8	338.1	293.7	419.0
Concrete Slabs (mn sq m)	1.06	1.43	1.91	1.91	1.78
Cement Blocks & Cable Cover (1,000 cu m)	18.1	55.9	51.4	50.6	36.1
Kerbstone (million M)*	0.86	1.21	1.20	0.94	0.05
Reinforced Concrete Pipes (1,000 metric tons)*	92.9	100.9	42.3	34.0	36.7
Circular Concrete Pipes (1,000 metric tons)*	186.1	215.5	173.0	106.5	24.7
Manhole Rings and Shafts (1,000 M)*	8.3	8.9	8.6	3.7	13.8
Ready Mixed Concrete (1,000 cu m)	63.3	49.3	43.0	67.8	87.9

*1982 quantity measure units have been changed from meter to cubic meter

Source: Kuwait Annual Statistical Abstract 1983

AGRICULTURE AND FISHING

Table 44.

LAND UTILIZATION
(Dunums)

	1977/78	1978/79	1979/80	1980/81
Crops	11,173	11,071	13,511	20,666
Trees	22,689	22,689	22,689	24,220
Pastures	17,179,100	17,179,100	17,179,100	17,179,100
Unused Cultivable Land	164,628	164,730	162,290	153,604
Non-Cultivable Land	440,410	440,410	440,410	440,410

Source: Kuwait Annual Statistical Abstract 1983.

Table 45.

PRODUCTION OF CROPS QUANTITY AND VALUES

	Quantity Crop Production (in tons)			**Value of Crop Production** (thousand KD)		
Crop	1978/79	1979/80	1980/81	1978/79	1979/80	1980/81
Winter Crops:						
Fruits	11,718	12,396	15,510	713.6	1,331.2	1,111.2
Leafy	5,216	6,837	8,844	617.0	767.1	1,077.6
Tuberous	8,189	9,100	9,813	926.9	1,246.1	914.2
Pulses	25	107	88	4.1	17.3	9.5
Various Vegetables	244	35	88	22.9	13.0	19.8
Total Winter Vegetables	25,392	28,475	34,343	2,284.5	3,374.7	3,132.3
Others	207	198	467	41.2	14.9	57.9
Total	25,599	28,673	34,810	2,325.7	3,389.6	3,190.2
Summer Crops:						
Fruits	3,221	4,342	3,898	216.8	376.7	432.7
Leafy	2,904	3,740	3,012	304.1	416.8	245.7
Others	39	27	11	2.3	3.5	2.3
Total	6,164	8,109	6,921	523.2	797.0	680.7
Semi-perennial Crops	25,631	36,585	90,399	1,159.4	1,688.7	4,396.0
Grand Total	**57,394**	**73,367**	**132,130**	**4,008.3**	**5,875.3**	**8,266.9**

Source: Kuwait Annual Statistical Abstract 1983

Table 46.

AREA CULTIVATED
(Dunums)

Crop	1978/79	1979/80	1980/81
Winter Crops:			
Fruits	4,697	5,013	6,222
Leafy	911	1,176	1,494
Tuberous	3,031	3,556	2,605
Pulses	17	70	57
Various Vegetables	102	33	70
Total Winter Vegetables	8,758	9,848	10,448
Others	688	656	1,503
Total Winter Crops	**9,446**	**10,504**	**11,951**
Summer Crops:			
Fruits	1,720	2,189	2,177
Leafy	514	786	537
Others	25	55	7
Total Summer Crops	**2,259**	**3,030**	**2,721**
Semi-perennial Crops	1,982	2,830	6,985
Grand Total	**13,687**	**16,364**	**21,657**

Source: Kuwait Annual Statistical Abstract 1983

Table 47.

VALUE OF ANIMAL PRODUCTION
(Thousand KD)

	1976/77	1977/78	1978/79	1979/80	1980/81
Sheep and goat meat	1,445	1,661	3,042	3,658	4,769
Beef	312	385	551	892	202
Poultry meat	5,526	4,817	7,823	5,098	8,494
Milk	2,555	6,126	7,767	8,921	2,349
Eggs	1,369	1,498	4,529	5,788	7,874
Wool, hair and leather	77	102	174	279	431
Total animal production	11,284	14,589	23,886	24,636	24,119
Fishing	3,310	4,240	3,801	3,688	8,453
Total Agricultural Income	17,771	22,073	31,804	34,355	41,052

Source: Kuwait Annual Statistical Abstract 1983

Table 48.

LIVESTOCK AND POULTRY IN HOLDINGS

Indicator	1976/77	1977/78	1978/79	1979/80	1980/81
Capital Governorate					
Cattle	179	146	243	--	--
Sheep	6,991	2,502	6,415	--	--
Goats	910	744	644	--	--
Poultry	239,952	211,705	408,102	300	--
Hawalli Governorate					
Cattle	5,266	5,588	4,904	6,133	10
Sheep	15,557	10,456	11,164	41,709	76,709
Goats	429	337	330	498	--
Poultry	596,790	603,379	428,016	367,661	374,500
Ahmadi Governorate					
Cattle	173	207	242	264	212
Sheep	6,099	1,570	3,454	8,979	10,198
Goats	898	560	861	1,420	1,182
Poultry	541,677	690,308	595,472	578,565	2,057,413
Jahra Governorate					
Cattle	--	--	--	161	7,064
Sheep	--	--	--	9,362	166,246
Goats	--	--	--	976	10,739
Poultry	--	--	--	820,920	9,595,697
(Al-Jahra Governorate established in 1980)					
Total					
Cattle	5,618	5,941	5,389	6,558	7,286
Sheep	28,647	14,528	21,033	60,050	253,153
Goats	2,237	1,641	1,835	2,894	11,921
Poultry	1,377,619	1,505,392	1,431,590	1,767,446	12,027,610

Source: Kuwait Annual Statistical Abstract 1983

TRADE

Table 49.

BALANCE OF PAYMENTS
(Million $US)

	1978	1979	1980	1981	1982
Exports (fob)	10,234	18,114	21,062	15,682	10,670
Imports (fob)	-4,326	-4,870	-6,756	-6,736	-7,169
Net Services	1,023	1,516	4,273	6,697	3,560
Private transfers	-433	-532	-692	-689	-702
Official transfers	-800	-756	-888	-875	-573
Balance on Current Account	6,191	14,206	16,999	13,703	5,786
Direct Investment	-95	188	-407	36	-222
Portfolio Investment	-65	-586	-329	-291	108
Other Long Term Capital	-345	-94	699	248	-146
Other Short Term Capital	-531	65	-932	-829	-2,313
Net Errors and Omissions	-999	-4,074	-3,520	-3,179	-1,235

Source: IMF International Financial Statistics

Table 50.

BALANCE OF PAYMENTS SUMMARY
1980 – 83
(Million KD)

Current Receipts	**7,177**	**-27.2**	**5,222**	**-2.4**	**5,096**
Exports:	4,446	-29.8	3,121	3.8	3,239
Oil	3,888	-34.6	2,541	8.5	2,757
Other	558	3.9	580	-16.9	482
Investment Income	2,343	-21.8	1,831	-14.2	1,571
Other	388	-30.4	270	5.9	286
Current Payments:	**-3,086**	**20.1**	**-3,707**	**-3.9**	**-3,562**
Imports	-1,878	19.1	-2,236	-9.0	-2,035
Others	-1,208	21.8	-1,471	3.8	-1,527
Current Surplus	**4,091**	**-63.0**	**1,515**	**1.3**	**1,534**
Capital Account	**-2,585**		**224**		**-456**
Government Investment	-2,214		6		150
Other (net)	-371		218		-606
Errors and Omissions	-1,428		-1,174		-1,264
Overall Surplus	**78**		**565**		**-186**

Source: Central Bank of Kuwait

Table 51.

TRADE BY COMMODITY SECTIONS
(Percent of total)

Item	1977	1978	1979	1980	1981*
Exports					
Food, Beverages & Tobacco	.6	.6	.4	.5	.1
Raw Materials excl. Fuels	.2	.2	.3	.2	--
Fuels	88.4	88.6	89.8	88.9	87.6
Manufactured Goods	10.9	10.6	9.5	10.4	10.1
Imports					
Food, Beverages & Tobacco	11.7	14.3	15.3	14.3	14.5
Raw Materials excl. Fuels	1.7	2.1	2.3	2.0	1.5
Fuels	.7	.6	.7	.8	.5
Manufactured Goods	85.1	82.2	80.6	82.3	79.2/1

* Figures for 1981 derived from Ministry of Planning,Central Statistical Office data.
/1 Manufactured goods here includes machinery and transport equipment.

Source: International Financial Statistics Supplement No. 4, 1982

Table 52.

KUWAIT'S TERMS OF TRADE
(1975 = 100)

	1979	1980	1981	1982	1983*
Export price index	176.5	284.0	327.1	307.8	265.0
Import price index	158.2	170.4	170.8	161.9	155.8
Terms of Trade	111.6	166.6	191.5	190.1	170.1
Percent change	34.6	49.3	14.9	-0.7	-10.5

* Figures represent Jan-Sept data only.

Source: International Financial Statistics Supplement No. 4, 1982

Table 53.

MAIN TRADING PARTNERS
(Imports by Country of Origin)
As Percent of Total

	1977	1978	1979	1980	1981
Asia and Oceania	41.5	38.4	38.8	40.2	39.7
Japan	19.8	19.5	18.3	19.9	22.7
India	3.8	3.4	3.3	3.4	2.2
Korea, Rep. of	6.0	2.9	3.3	3.7	2.8
China, P.R.	2.7	2.1	2.5	1.6	1.9
Taiwan	2.4	2.8	2.9	3.1	2.6
Other	6.8	7.7	8.5	8.5	7.5
Western Europe	37.4	39.9	37.6	39.0	38.8
United Kingdom	9.9	10.2	10.0	9.2	7.8
West Germany	9.3	9.1	8.0	7.9	11.9
Italy	5.0	6.3	5.6	6.3	5.8
France	3.0	3.7	3.4	5.1	3.5
Other	10.2	10.6	10.6	10.5	9.8
Western Hemisphere	15.4	14.8	16.8	15.1	16.3
United States	13.6	13.2	14.5	12.9	13.9
Other	1.8	1.6	2.3	2.2	2.4
Middle East and Africa	2.6	3.9	4.2	3.8	3.5
Lebanon	1.0	1.4	1.2	1.2	1.1
Other	1.6	2.5	3.0	2.6	2.4
Eastern Europe	3.1	3.0	2.6	1.9	1.7
Total	100.0	100.0	100.0	100.0	100.0

1981 figures derived from Ministry of Planning, Central Statistical Office data.

Source: Central Bank of Kuwait, Ministry of Planning.

Table 54.

KUWAIT'S BALANCE OF TRADE WITH MAJOR INTERNATIONAL GROUPS
(as percent of total)

	1977	1978	1979	1980	1981
Industrial Countries	45.7	52.4	57.7	37.5	17.9
USA	-9.9	-9.0	-4.8	-5.3	-9.8
Japan	30.2	28.9	28.3	17.3	24.4
EEC	24.9	33.5	33.4	23.0	2.7
Other 1/	0.5	-1.0	0.8	2.5	0.6
Other European Countries 2/	-0.6	-0.8	-0.1	-0.3	0.4
European Socialist Countries	-0.7	-0.6	-1.0	0.2	-2.5
Arab Countries	15.1	12.4	9.0	10.2	22.0
Saudi Arabia	8.7	6.9	3.2	3.6	5.8
United Arab Emirates	1.9	1.2	1.1	1.1	2.1
Lebanon	-0.6	-0.7	-0.3	-0.4	-0.7
Iraq	0.7	1.6	1.7	3.1	10.9
Other	4.4	3.3	3.3	2.8	3.9
Other Countries	40.5	36.6	34.4	52.4	59.1

1/ Includes Canada,Oceania,Austria, Finland, Iceland, Norway, Sweden, Switzerland, and Spain

2/ Includes Portugal, Andorra, Gibralter, Malta, Yugoslavia, Greece.

Source: Central Bank of Kuwait compiled from data of Ministry of Planning, Central Statistical Office "Foreign Trade Bulletins"

Table 55.

DESTINATION OF EXPORTS AND RE-EXPORTS
(as percent of total)

	1977	1978	1979	1980	1981*
Asia and Oceania	49.5	49.4	50.8	50.8	60.9
Japan	25.1	24.8	24.1	13.5	23.7
Korea, Rep. of	6.6	6.6	6.6	7.5	8.1
Taiwan	6.7	6.5	6.2	8.8	11.5
Singapore	1.2	1.2	4.5	7.5	3.6
Other	9.9	10.3	9.4	13.5	14.0
Western Europe	29.8	34.7	33.2	34.8	17.1
Netherlands	7.2	9.0	10.8	12.1	6.6
United Kingdom	8.9	8.7	6.4	11.6	4.3
France	3.1	2.4	3.2	5.2	1.8
Italy	6.7	9.1	8.7	1.6	1.7
Other	3.9	5.5	4.1	4.3	2.7
Western Hemisphere	8.4	4.1	3.3	5.6	2.9
Brazil	5.6	3.0	1.9	0.8	2.0
United States	1.8	0.7	0.6	2.4	0.4
Other	1.0	0.4	0.8	2.4	0.5
Middle East and Africa	9.0	8.7	9.7	6.5	14.2
Saudi Arabia	4.4	3.9	2.4	2.1	0.1
Iraq	N.A.	0.9	1.3	2.1	6.3
Other	4.6	4.8	7.3	4.4	7.8
Eastern Europe	1.2	1.0	--	--	1.0
Total	**100.0**	**100.0**	**100.0**	**100.0**	**96.1**

* 1981 figures derived from Central Statistical Office data. Totals do not equal 100 due to the omission of ship stores and bunkers which account for 1.8% and articles going to an unspecified destination which account for 2% of total exports.

Source: Central Bank of Kuwait, Ministry of Planning.

LABOR

Table 56.

LABOR FORCE PARTICIPATION RATES (1980)

Year	Females(%)	Males(%)	Total(%)
Kuwaiti	5.1	34.1	19.4
Non-Kuwaiti	16.6	66.2	47.8

Source: Ministry of Planning Central Statistical Office

Table 57.

ECONOMICALLY ACTIVE POPULATION
(1980 census)

	Kuwaitis	**Non-Kuwaitis**	**Total**
Agriculture, hunting, and tishing	3,983	5,212	9,150
Mining and quarrying	2,397	4,262	6,659
Manufacturing industries	3,179	38,081	41,260
Electricity, gas and water	2,068	6,099	8,167
Construction	1,206	95,893	97,099
Trade and restaurants	4,577	53,840	58,417
Transport, storage and communications	7,832	22,321	30,153
Financial institutions, insurance	2,816	9,870	12,686
Services (including defence)	75,461	144,992	220,453
Total	**103,474**	**380,570**	**484,033**

Memo Item
Average growth of labor force: 4.1% (1970 - 1980)

Source: The Middle East and North Africa 1983-84

TRANSPORTATION AND COMMUNICATIONS

Table 58.

TRANSPORTATION INFRASTRUCTURE

Kilometers of road:	2,000 km of all-weather highways.
List of ports:	Shuwaikh Shuaib Mina al-Ahmadi
Oil tanker fleet:	8 carriers for crude oil 4 for Liquid Petroleum Gas 3 for oil products
Private shipping companies:	
Kuwait Oil Tankers Co.	7 vessels 1,157,000 tons 3 tankers 983,000 tons
Kuwait Shipping Co.	40 vessels 920,000 tons
National Airline:	Kuwait Airways Corporation
Equipment:	11 Boeings
Number of airfields:	11 (Kuwait City with 2,500 m of runway; 6 usuable and 4 with permanent surface runways.)

Table 59.

REGISTERED VEHICLES IN USE
(1,000 units)

Type in Use at End of Year	1978	1979	1980	1981	1982
Private Cars	312.0	353.7	389.3	425.6	469.1
Taxis	9.0	9.6	9.7	9.7	9.7
Private Trucks	71.7	81.2	88.5	94.5	103.6
Private Buses	5.1	5.6	6.0	6.4	7.0
Public Buses	2.0	2.2	2.4	2.8	3.3
Total *	**439.6**	**496.6**	**543.0**	**590.5**	**667.9**
Registered During the Year	**1978**	**1979**	**1980**	**1981**	**1982**
Private Cars	49.1	47.1	42.9	44.4	50.6
Taxis	1.1	.6	.3	.2	.1
Private Trucks	14.4	11.1	9.2	7.4	11.4
Public Trucks	3.6	4.9	3.2	4.7	4.8
Private Buses	.7	.5	.6	.5	.7
Public Buses	.1	.2	.1	.4	.5
Total	**69.9**	**64.4**	**56.3**	**57.6**	**69.1***

* Includes motorcycles

Source: Kuwait Annual Statistical Abstract 1983

Table 60.

PRINCIPAL DAILY NEWSPAPERS

Name	Circulation
Al-Anba (Arabic)	55,000
Al-Qabas (Arabic)	75,000
Al-Rai al Amm (Arabic)	50,000
Al-Siyasa (Arabic)	80,000
Al-Watan (Arabic)	58,000
Arab Times (English)	42,000
Kuwait Times (English)	28,000
Number of radio receivers (1981):	525,000
Number of televisions (1981):	542,000
Number of telephones (1982):	191,605

HEALTH, EDUCATION AND WELFARE

Table 61.

HEALTH ESTABLISHMENTS AND PERSONNEL
PUBLIC HOSPITALS, CLINICS, AND MEDICAL STAFF

Item	1978	1979	1980	1981	1982
HospitalS & Sanitoria	10	9	11	14	15
Clinics	48	49	53	55	54
Dental Clinics	70	78	94	105	114
Maternal Care Centers	15	15	18	17	18
Child Care Centers	22	24	28	28	28
Preventive Health Centers	15	16	23	23	23
School Clinics	383	420	457	480	494
Medical Staff:					
Physicians	1,388	1,555	1,921	2,133	2,264
Dentists	140	167	181	203	223
Pharmacists	191	228	252	322	345
Asst. Phamacists	356	350	338	336	342
Therapists	105	144	185	202	202
Health Officers	179	223	--	210	230
Quarantine Officers	139	140	--	206	--
Laboratory Assistants	487	567	661	806	860
Dental Technicians	55	51	56	55	70
Qualified Nurses	3,891	3,882	5,407	6,128	6,251
Assistant Nurses	345	501	385	323	596
Radiographers	229	263	329	423	438
Male Nurses	1,004	939	918	1,101	1,019

Source: Kuwait Annual Statistical Abstract 1983

EDUCATION

Literacy rate: 55%
Education is free, universal, compulsory from 6-14
Academic year: September to May

Table 62.

STUDENTS AT GOVERNMENT SCHOOLS BY SEX & LEVEL OF EDUCATION

	1978/79	1979/80	1980/81	1981/82	1982/83
Kindergarten:					
Male	8,349	8,611	9,103	10,134	10,954
Female	7,850	8,203	8,667	9,628	10,334
Total	16,199	16,814	17,770	19,762	21,287
Primary:					
Male	62,303	64,269	64,876	66,370	63,014
Female	54,418	57,969	60,238	63,014	63,338
Total	116,721	122,238	125,114	129,384	128,712
Intermediate:					
Male	47,159	51,291	55,409	59,554	61,609
Female	38,430	41,280	45,209	49,127	51,615
Total	85,589	92,571	100,681	108,681	113,224
Secondary:					
Male	22,180	24,711	27,506	30,091	33,270
Female	20,928	22,565	24,454	26,455	29,413
Total	43,108	47,276	51,960	56,546	62,683
Vocational:					
Male	869	2,050	2,432	3,068	3,672
Female	739	1,951	2,303	2,682	3,101
Total	1,608	4,001	4,735	5,750	6,773
Others:					
Male	2,726	1,724	1,661	1,595	1,489
Female	1,567	709	752	794	774
Total	4,293	2,433	2,413	2,389	2,263
Total:					
Male	143,586	152,656	160,987	170,812	176,368
Female	123,932	132,677	141,623	151,700	158,574
Total	**267,518**	**285,333**	**302,610**	**322,512**	**334,942**

Source: Kuwait Annual Statistical Abstract 1983

Table 63.

ENROLLMENT IN PRIVATE EDUCATIONAL INSTITUTIONS AND KUWAIT UNIVERSITY

Private Arab Schools (1982/83):	**Enrollments**	**Number of Establishments**
Total	45,826	105
Kindergarten	9,240	26
Primary	18,448	32
Intermediate	10,255	26
Secondary	7,883	21
Private Foreign Schools (1982/83):		
Total	29,437	95
Kindergarten	4,569	25
Primary	13,028	27
Intermediate	9,573	26
Secondary	4,971	17
Kuwait University (1982/83):		
Undergraduates	11,949	
Kuwaiti Nationals	8,656	
Men	3,638	
Women	5,018	
Other Nationalities	3,293	

Source: Kuwait Annual Statistical Abstract 1983

Table 64.

KUWAIT STUDENTS STUDYING ABROAD

	1980-81			**1981-82**			**1982-83**		
	Male	**Female**	**Total**	**Male**	**Female**	**Total**	**Male**	**Female**	**Total**
Egypt	371	207	578	267	128	395	205	78	283
Lebanon	237	42	279	6	13	19	441	58	499
Iraq	4	3	7	4	4	8	4	5	9
UK	187	32	219	144	8	152	74	3	77
USA	1,314	42	1,356	1,439	28	1,467	1,426	23	1,449
France	10	16	26	11	20	31	31	35	66
Pakistan	9	3	12	8	4	12	37	5	42
USSR	1	-	1	-	-	-	-	-	-
Other	214	41	255	131	21	152	73	33	106
Total	**2,347**	**386**	**2,733**	**2,010**	**226**	**2,236**	**2,438**	**244**	**2,682**

Source: Kuwait Annual Statistical Abstract 1983

Table 66.

CURRENT HOUSING SITUATIONS

Buildings (1980):	106,663
Dwellings (1980):	180,400
Households (1980):	196,174
Standard units distributed by Government to lower income groups in 1979 (1979):	3,378

Source: Kuwait Ministry of Planning Central Statistical Office

Table 65.

HOUSING SCHEMES TO BE COMPLETED BY 1986

Project	Average Income		Low Income	
	Apts.	Villas	Apts.	Villas
Failaka				70
West Agaila				2,541
Ardiya II				2,364
Jahra II		330		1,720
Sabah al-Salem		1,990	874	
Sawaber	951			
Northeast Sawaber	368			
East Sulaibikhat	2,000			
Fintas				3,480
Funaitis and South Sabah al-Salem		5,632		14,080
Total	**3,319**	**7,952**	**874**	**24,255**

Source: National Housing Authority 1981 Annual Report

Table 67.

VALUE OF GOVERNMENT WELFARE PAYMENTS (1982)

	Number of Recipients	Value in '000 KD
Disability	1,550	646
Old age	4,553	2,527
Students families	147	75
Sickness	741	329
Widowhood	3,469	1,900
Divorce	3,818	2,212
Orphanage	984	567
Financial difficulty	1,288	454
Imprisonment of supporter	741	308

Source: Kuwait Annual Statistical Absract 1983